One Man or Another:

Moving On

Shonda Lawrence, Ph.D.

One Man or Another: Moving On

ISBN 978-0-615-46237-0

Warning—Disclaimer

To Janie,

Thanks for your
Support! Enjoy your
read!

Shonda

FOR

My children, Jasmine and Justin Wills. Thanks
for always believing in me.

Acknowledgments

It is with great pleasure that I write this book. Throughout this process there have been many ups and downs. There have been times I felt I knew exactly what I was doing and why I was doing it. There have been times I have questioned my ability to clearly illustrate on paper shared experiences and times I felt guilty for not putting as much effort into other areas of my life as I have this project. I thank God for giving me the strength and fortitude to realize my dream. I have been blessed to have in my life my mother, Geraldine Lawrence, nudging me along to dream the unthinkable; friends and confidants, Brenda Thomas, for making a quiet place for me to think; Sheryl Whitehead, Desiree Stepteau-Watson, Betty Reed, and Phyllis Hammond, for listening and hearing me. I am also so thankful for those of you who inspired me through your words, unwavering love and acts of kindness: Cheryl Lawrence, Lisa Galloway, Anderson M. Myles, III, Cleme Johnson, Cheryl Newsome, Yvette Cooper, Lynette Thomas, Rowlanda Howard, Lillian Jackson, Lenita Bushrod Black, Patricia Arnold, Candace Stoakley, Cassandra Grant, Renee Padgett, Billy Ray Golston, Wilson Malone, Anthony 'Speedy' Williams, A. Richard Wills, Jaiya John, Seth Hosick, James Crowley, and Ronald Moaton. Finally, I am most grateful to the very special men and women who inspired the creation of the characters in this book. I love you all and thank you from the bottom of my heart.

Table of Contents

JANICE

Carlton - The Maintenance Man

Carlton is a state employee with great benefits. His job is not demanding so he can get away whenever he wants and not be questioned about his whereabouts. He has a bachelor's degree and is a certified drug counselor. He has always been able to get and keep a decent paying job because his parents are deeply involved in city politics. In fact they are quite influential. They're not rich but are pillars of the community and influence a lot of votes.

Carlton can't really talk on a deep level about current issues but knows all about sports. He's a decent looking guy who grows on you. You know the kind. Six feet tall with a muscularly defined body, impeccable and expensive taste and always dressed to kill. Eventually you find features that are just "soooo" cute about him. He's reliable and always available. Whenever you see him out he's with a different woman who is just as well put together as he is.

I met Carlton at a small bar, which hosts some of the hottest musicians anywhere. The night I met Carlton "The Brand New Heavies" were playing. I was there with my boyfriend, Trent, and three other couples. We had planned the outing for months.   We had never even heard of the group but Kara's boyfriend convinced us we had not lived until we had gone to one of their concerts. So instead of going to see "Frankie Beverly and Maze" again, we love them and they always put on a fabulous show, we decided to try something different. The music was extraordinary.

My best friend, Kara, had to go to the restroom. As we were making our way through the crowd, I felt someone gently grab my hand. I turned and pulled my hand away. He said, "Hi, if you come back this way can I talk to you for a minute?" I replied, "Maybe" and kept walking toward the restroom. When we got in the restroom Kara started laughing and said, "O.K. hooker, don't even start. You know Mr. Insecure Trent is out there and if he sees you saying anything to anyone the rest of the evening is going to be a downer." I replied, "Forget that. You know I always keep my options open. Trent and I have a good relationship but maybe there's something better out there. Don't get me wrong, I'm not looking but if the opportunity should come a knocking I just might have to open that door." Kara just rolled her eyes and said, "Come on Ms. Hookerific. Let's go."

Kara purposely tried to lead us back to our seats in the opposite direction of the guy that grabbed my hand. She was walking really fast. I caught her by the arm and redirected our path right back to Mr. Possibility. He said, "I can see you're here with someone. I've been watching you all night. Here's my number. Call me when you can get free." He had written his name and number on a cocktail napkin and 'please call' in capital letters.

When we got back to the group Trent asked who the guy I was talking to was. Damn, how did he see that? I told him I didn't know the guy and he just asked if I was having a good time. End of story. Trent had every reason to be suspicious. You see although I cared about Trent very much, I was always looking for something else. I was twenty-seven years old and had never been faithful in any relationship I was in. Well maybe not relationships I was in. I would always break up with the guy, pursue my interest in another guy and if it didn't work go back to the guy I had broken up with. Whatever! Men did it all the time. I didn't blame them, women allowed it and apparently men did too. Trent and I had been dating for two and a half years and I had broken up with him three times, and went back to him three times.

We decided to go to the after party at a nearby hotel. When we arrived I saw Carlton again. He was handing his keys to the valet as he was opening the passenger side of the car. A woman got out. She was strikingly beautiful. They looked really good together. It was clear to me they were a couple and what he wanted from me was a little something on the side. This was right up my alley. No commitment or strings attached. Kara just looked at me and shook her head. We had been friends since second grade. She knew the look.

I called Carlton the next day. We talked for about twenty minutes and made plans to meet after work. We met at a restaurant on the other side of town. I told him all about Trent and my relationship. He didn't seem to have a problem with it. I asked him about the woman in the car. He said he didn't have a monogamous relationship and had a lot of friends with benefits. I asked him if he was looking to add me to his roster. He laughed and said, "You're here aren't you." I liked his style. He was straight forward and to the point. We talked on the phone and met for lunch a few more times. The meetings and conversations always included sexual innuendos. We talked about our sex lives, sexual fantasies, and what we liked and what we didn't like. By the third week I think we both had had enough of the talking.

We made plans to meet at a hotel. I paid for the hotel and Carlton brought food, wine, vodka, and a few more things to make the night everything we fantasized. I stopped by the kinky lingerie store before I got there. I planned to fulfill at least one of his fantasies if not more that night. I opened the hotel room door and

Carlton was already at the door as I opened it. He grabbed me and we started kissing. Our clothes were off in what seemed like a matter of seconds. We were all over that room. He was on top; I was on top, from one position to the next. We were on the bed, against the wall, on the floor, on the dresser, in the shower, everywhere. It was so hot. We slept, woke up and started again. We never ate or drank. The lingerie would have to wait until next time. As we were getting dressed we planned our next rendezvous.

When I got home I had three messages from Trent. He wanted me to meet him for dinner. I just couldn't. I wanted to lay in my bed alone, curl up under the sheets and bask in the afterglow of Carlton and me. I called Trent and told him I wasn't feeling well. He asked if I wanted to have lunch at his house the next day. Now I knew what that meant. Eat and then have sex. I told him I would see him at his house the next day. He was satisfied and said; "Feel better because I've been saving something up just for you." He started doing that devilish laugh he always did when he wanted to have sex. I was thinking yeah right if you only knew.

I went to Trent's the next day and as I suspected the same old routine. He ordered the shrimp and lobster pasta, had the wine chilled, and music playing. After we ate we sat on the couch and drank the rest of the bottle of wine. As usual, he started by kissing me on my neck, moving my hand back and forth over his crouch and saying, "Baby come on. It's all for you." I obliged him.

I was never one to turn down sex. I can only think of two times. One time the guy had what I termed a pencil and I really didn't want to be frustrated so I pretended I had to go to the restroom, got dressed and left. The other time, the guy was abnormally long and large and I didn't want to take the chance of him ripping my goodie-bag into pieces. I had a girlfriend who had to have surgery twice because her man was so large. He kept tilting her uterus out of place. She was in so much pain. I jumped up from the sofa and said, "I don't think so" and asked he leave my apartment.

Like I said, I loved having sex. I could have sex three to four times a day. The difference between me and other women was I had sex for the orgasm only. Not love or affection. After sex I didn't want to cuddle or caress. It was perfectly fine if my sex partner left. I preferred that. Trent had a hard time understanding it but he knew as soon as we were done I was out of there. He came to accept that was just who I was. I decided I wouldn't break up with Trent this time because the situation was exactly the way I wanted it. I didn't have to. There was the secret of Carlton and I and then there was my real relationship with Trent.

Trent was tall and very handsome. All in all he was just a good guy. I knew he loved me and on some level I loved him. I just wasn't ready to make a commitment. He treated me well. If there was anything I ever needed he was always there. Sometimes he would just do things without me even asking. He would say, I saw you were running low on food so I brought you some groceries, or I changed the blown light in the hallway, or I was at the phone company to pay my bill so I paid yours too. None of his friends liked me. They all thought he could do better. He told me he could tell they thought he was a fool and they would say to him I treated him like shit. I was as good to Trent as I could be at that time in my life. He always had a choice to leave but never did.

Over the next few weeks Carlton and I continued to meet at the hotel. The sex always felt like it was the first time. Around the third month into our indiscretion, Carlton asked me to meet him at his house. I didn't think anything of it. Maybe he just wanted to change up the scenery. I got his address and made my way to his house. When I pulled up I thought wow what a nice home. It was a brick bungalow with a well-maintained yard in a very nice neighborhood. I rang the doorbell. An older woman answered the door. I asked for Carlton. She told me to come in and go down to the basement. Although she showed me the way, you could tell she was perturbed by my intrusion.

As I walked down the stairs, I saw Carlton sitting with what I thought was a couple. He introduced them as his sister and his friend. I smiled and shook their hands and said, "Really nice to meet you both." In my mind, I was thinking what the hell is going on. I really don't want to meet anyone. This was supposed to be something between us. What if one of them knows Trent or one of his friends? This is definitely not cool. Does he live in his parent's basement? No wonder he can afford the expensive car and clothes. I couldn't wait for them to leave so I could talk to Carlton about what he was thinking by putting me in this situation. Carlton's sister only stayed a few minutes before she left. After about an hour Carlton had to ask his friend to leave. Finally, we could talk.

Carlton and I were sitting on a bed. He immediately started undressing me. I stood up and stepped back and asked, "Is this where you live?" He replied, "Yeah, come back over here." I asked, "Is this your home or your parent's home?" He replied, "This is the rundown. I live here with my parents. I live in the basement. I save a lot of money. When I have enough I'm going to buy the house I want not the one I can get based on my salary. I want to pay cash for it or most of it. My sister is still in college so she still lives here. I help her with her tuition. It takes the strain off my parents. I don't pay rent or any other bills here. My boy came by unexpectedly and my sister likes him so whenever he's around she breaks her neck to strike up any ole conversation with him. Now are we going to do this or what?"

I always liked that Carlton was straightforward but what he had just told me didn't sit well with me. I decided to have sex with him and not see him anymore. I pulled out all the tricks. This was going to be the last time. We fell asleep. When I woke up, I got dressed. I shook Carlton to wake him and let him know I was leaving. He walked me to the front door. It was pitch black outside. I looked back at the door of Carlton's parent's house and Carlton was closing the door. He didn't even wait to see if I was in the car safely. I thought how unconcerned, inconsiderate and rude. That was confirmation enough for me. Carlton and I were over. Whatever! It was a nice run.

About three days later I was burning and itching like nobody's business down there. I had a thick discharge. Please don't let this be happening. Could Carlton have given me a sexually transmitted disease? I had to go to the doctor immediately. I called my gynecologist. He couldn't see me until the next day. I called Carlton and asked him to meet me at the restaurant. He was more than willing to do so. We met and I must say he was looking and smelling good. He said, "I made the hotel reservation." I replied, "Cancel them. What nasty bitch have you been fucking? I've got something. I'm going to the doctor tomorrow and I'll let you know." As I proceeded to get up to leave, Carlton grabbed my arm and firmly said, "Sit your ass down. You can't talk to me like that. Since we've been kicking it I haven't slept with anyone else. You know how often we meet. You were there. Besides we always used protection. Now if you're itching and your coochie's broke, you need to check with Tim." I said, "Trent." Carlton said, "Tim, Trent, whatever his damn name is. But don't come in here accusing me of some shit I have nothing to do with." I stood up, looked Carlton dead in the eyes and said, "Lose my number" and walked away.

I went to the gynecologist and was told I had a severe yeast infection. I was so relieved. That could be fixed. While I was there I was tested for other STD's, had a breast exam and a pregnancy test. I called Kara while I was sitting waiting for the doctor to return to the examining room. We were so happy about the results. I had never had a scare like that before. I was nervous all the day before, into the night and up until the doctor came back with the results. I was more than scared I was petrified. My mind was running away with thoughts of dying with one disease or the other. Kara said it was a wakeup call. We agreed I would have to change my whorish ways. We laughed.

Kara asked if Trent and I were going to be able to make it to her dinner party. Just as I was saying, "no doubt, we've got a lot to celebrate" my doctor walked into the room. I told Kara I would call her back. He told me to get dressed and he'd be back in a couple of minutes to discuss the results of the tests. I was putting on my shoes when the doctor returned. He said, "All of the tests are negative for STD's which is very good because you're pregnant. You are approximately fourteen weeks along. I'm going to prescribe prenatal vitamins and I want to schedule you for blood work. Make sure you see the nurse. Do you have any questions?"

I couldn't talk. I sat there dumbfounded for a few minutes. Me, pregnant? What? My menstrual period had always been very irregular. Sometimes I would go three and four months without one. Why was he saying this? I hated him! I got hot all over. My heart was racing. I was sweating. I felt nauseous. It was if I was having an out of body experience. I could barely hear the doctor talking. I remember him calling the nurse; a girl Kara and I had gone to high school with. The nurse came in and somehow I ended up on the examination table. I felt weak; faint even. All of a sudden, Kara was in the room trying to get me to drink a sip of water.

The nurse had called Kara because she knew we were friends. She used my cell phone to call Kara to ask if she could come to the doctor's office to drive me home. When Kara got the phone call she was totally baffled. We had just gotten off the phone laughing about the whole situation. After I drank a couple of sips of water, I was able to sit up. The doctor came back into the room and asked how I was feeling. He asked to speak to me alone about alternatives. I told him to please let Kara stay. He said, "O.k. if it's fine with you it's fine with me. I have never had a patient react to being pregnant the way you have." Before I could respond, Kara burst into laughter and tears at the same time. Both the doctor and I just looked at her. She couldn't contain herself so she left the room. The doctor began to talk about alternatives but I stopped him and said, "I think I've had enough for one day. I'll just schedule an appointment for next week if that's o.k." I walked out the room. Kara was sitting in the waiting area. She ran towards me and hugged me really tight and said, "I'll go with you to the abortion clinic." I started crying and said, "I can't do it." We left the office, got in separate cars and talked and cried on our cell phones all the way to my apartment.

I didn't know what I was going to do? All kinds of thoughts were running through my head. I didn't want a baby. Maybe I could put aside my beliefs about abortion and get rid of it. I didn't even like children like that. Sure, I didn't want anyone to hurt children. I was sad for a moment when I saw hungry children on television. I donated to Save the Children and

Children's International but I also donated to the Animal Rescue League. I babysat sometimes but I knew the children would eventually go home. I saw my nieces and nephew on birthdays and holidays for a little while. They were cute and lovable but I didn't want to see them all the time. What about my body? I worked hard to keep it tight. Now some alien form would enter my body and grow it all out of shape. The bigger ah ha was whose baby was it? On second thought this didn't have to be a problem. It was Trent's baby. He was reliable, considerate, caring and would make a great father. I didn't know what to do. Trent never said he wanted children. In fact, he was rather awkward around children. I didn't know if I wanted to be tied to Trent for the rest of my life? I thought, 'Was I being punished?'

Kara and I cried and talked for hours. Kara's boyfriend and Trent must have called a total of ten times between the both of them. We turned our phones off and talked more. I decided to be honest with Trent. The next day was Kara's dinner party. I didn't want to ruin it so I decided to tell Trent about the baby after the party. I was nervous and antsy the whole time we were at the party. After we ate I told Kara I needed to leave. I couldn't take it anymore. Of course she understood. Trent and I got our coats and went back to my place. It took everything I had in me to muster up the nerve to tell Trent I was pregnant.

We were still hungry so I made guacamole dip. Kara wasn't a good cook but always wanted to give a dinner party for her friends and insisted on cooking. We indulged her but always knew we would have to eat when we left. I sat the dip on the table and went back to the kitchen to get the tortilla chips. While I was in the kitchen I turned it over and over in my mind how I would tell Trent. Before I never had a problem telling Trent anything because I felt I was in control. This was different. I had blundered big time. I returned to the dining room with the chips and all the planning about how I would tell Trent I was pregnant went out the window. I just blurted it out as I was opening the bag of chips.

We just stood there staring at each other. I could feel the tears welling up in my eyes. Trent walked toward me, smiled a big smile and said; "Now you have to marry me." I gently pushed him away from me and said, "I don't know if it's yours." Trent's smile disappeared and all you could see and feel was pure hurt and disappointment. It was the worst feeling in the world. He didn't say a word. He got his coat and left. I lay on the couch and cried myself to sleep. I hated being in this position.

The next morning Kara was ringing my doorbell. I could barely see from all of the crying. My eyes were just about swollen shut. I went to the door and Kara rushed in and asked, "Did you tell Trent the truth?" Apparently, Trent had called Kara's boyfriend and asked him to make a run with him. Kara said Trent and her boyfriend were on their way to a jewelry store to look at engagement rings. What? I assured Kara I had told Trent the truth. I couldn't believe it. After all I had done he still wanted to be with me. A couple of days later Trent called and asked if he could come by. I told him he could. When he arrived he had flowers and sparkling cider. He asked me to marry him. He had chosen the most beautiful ring. I said yes and we were married in Las Vegas three weeks later. I never thought my life would take this path but it did.

Although Trent treated me like a queen during my pregnancy, I hated being pregnant. After the baby was born, Trent could have won the "best father of the first six months" award if one existed. He got up in the middle of the night to feed and change the baby and came straight home after work to make sure the baby and I had everything we needed. He was attentive to our every whim. It wasn't until I returned to work things began to get ugly. Trent wasn't coming home right after work anymore. I was solely responsible for all of our son's needs. The tables had turned. Right after our son's first birthday, I learned Trent had been involved in two extramarital affairs. I took the information with stride. After all, I put him through a lot. I felt he was owed that. However, learning Trent impregnated an eighteen year old girl down the street from where we lived was more than I could bear. The girl had an abortion. I think I was more upset he had not worn protection during his indiscretion than him cheating on me.   In a way, this discretion cleared my conscience to do what I wanted to do anyway. I called Carlton.

Carlton seemed happy to hear from me. We met and soon afterwards resumed our scheduled rendezvous'. Now this was more like it. Trent and I rarely slept together over the next two years.   We were happiest when we were together as a family with our son. One on one didn't work for us. One day Trent called and asked that I leave work early because he really needed to talk to me. He said it was urgent and couldn't wait. When I got home there was a woman in our living room standing next to Trent. All I could think was this was his woman and he was going to ask me for a divorce. Strangely, I was very calm and braced myself for the possibility this might in fact be the case.

Trent said, "Baby, this is Dr. Guilliam. She is a marriage counselor. I invited her here because our marriage is in trouble and we need help." I was outraged but I tried to act as if it didn't bother me. I said, "Hello. Now what exactly has my wonderful husband been telling you?" Trent knew from that statement I was upset. I felt ambushed. Dr. Guilliam began to talk. She said, "I know this has probably taken you by surprise. I don't usually do this but

Trent is a friend of my husband's so I agreed to come here today. If you don't want to talk to me maybe I can refer you to someone else. If you don't want to talk today maybe we can schedule an appointment in my office. I don't want you to feel put upon." I replied, "No it's fine. Let's talk."

Dr. Guilliam said, "Good. Well to answer your question Trent hasn't told me much only he loves you and doesn't want to lose you. Do you feel your marriage is in trouble and, if so, are you willing to work on it?" I replied, "Everything's good for me but if Trent thinks we need to work on some things then I'm willing to listen to what you and Trent have to say." Dr. Guilliam replied, "Yes, but do you want to work on your marriage?" I told her to let me think about it and if so we would make an appointment to see her. She left. I was so mad at Trent. I couldn't speak. I didn't talk to him for two days.

On the third day, Kara came by with her husband, the same guy she had dated for years. Their coming by forced me into a situation where I would have to talk to Trent. Kara suggested we play a game. We decided to play scrabble. We hadn't played in a very long time. When we played scrabble you had to use your word in a sentence in order to get points. Kara and I were killing it. Trent didn't seem to be into the game. He had tiles that would gain him points but he never used them. Around about the fifth game

Trent finally spelled a word. It was C-A-R-L-T-O-N. I just looked at him and said, "You can't use that." He said, "Using it in a sentence, I know all about him and knew about him before we were married." Kara and her husband saw the writing on the wall and scurried to get out of there.

     After Kara and her husband left, Trent said, "Can we talk now?" I just looked at him with tears rolling down my face and said, "What? What is it?" He said, "I love you. If you don't love me tell me now. I'm tired. I can't do this anymore. I'm tired." We talked into the night and all the next day. We scheduled an appointment to talk to Dr. Guilliam. We worked things out. Of course, I had a lot more to work on than Trent. I even went to see a sex therapist. Yes, my issues went far and deep. My cousin had molested me when I was six. He was thirteen. It only happened once. After he raped me, we both cried. I was hurt physically and emotionally and he was sorry. I never said anything to anyone. Neither he nor I ever talked about it. I think something changed in me that day. In the process of healing, my therapist said I would eventually have to confront my cousin about what happened. This was difficult. It wasn't just my cousin I confronted; it was my immediate and extended family. Their reaction was just what I expected. My mother was furious with me because she had always made every effort to create an atmosphere where her children would be able to tell her anything and years later I was slapping her in the face with this. My cousin said he didn't remember anything like that happening but if it did he was sorry. Overall, the general consensus was if I didn't say anything about it then why bring it up now and cause dissention in the family. I was resolved to being satisfied with the fact that the ordeal was no longer a secret. That alone helped me to become a better me.

I stopped seeing Carlton and Trent stopped messing around with other women. Trent and I have been married for fifteen years. We did not have more children. Today, I can truly say I love Trent and I know he loves me. I would have never thought I would be as happy as I am now in a monogamous relationship. Who would have ever thought?

Insight

Trent loved me from the very beginning. I ignored him and had little consideration for his feelings. It was all about me. Instant gratification was what I desired and what I lived for. Even when I found out I was pregnant I wasn't capable of connecting with the life growing inside of me. My pregnancy was an imposition. I built walls around my heart. Trent unsuccessfully tried and tried again to break through. In the end, I realized I had pushed a good man to his breaking point for no other reason than I could. I took his love for granted.

I was incapable of anything else until I dealt with my own childhood issues that left me hard and cold inside.

Trent loved me through it all but years of subjecting himself to my abuse had to come out in some way. He cheated. He wanted to hurt me as much as I had hurt him and in the process he was losing himself. He realized his destructive behavior was destroying who he really was. It wasn't until he confronted me and I thought I was going to lose him that I knew how much he meant to me. Even when I thought he was going to ask me for a divorce with his new woman standing by his side, I still felt confident I could get him back if I wanted to. We wasted a lot of time with foolishness and dodging the real issues. Carlton wasn't the answer to what I needed. He was a distraction and as crazy as it may sound he was my security. Just think I almost let the maintenance man destroy Trent, our family and me.

RITA

John - The I Gotta Get Paid Man

John is six foot seven and commands attention when he enters a room. He is a good-looking man. He is the color of a fine rich dark chocolate with long eyelashes, perfect white teeth and model features. I met John at a nightclub. I was there with my girlfriend, Kayse.

There was a new club in the neighborhood. Kayse and I had missed the grand opening the previous weekend. We decided to check it out the following Saturday. Kayse and I went shopping for something to wear that night. We had just cashed our income tax refund checks. We were excited because we found a sale, which made it possible for us to buy a couple of outfits. Freshly done hair, nails, new outfits, and new purses, we were sooooo happy and we were going to look sooooo good. We couldn't wait to get all dolled up and hit the new club.

When we drove up we noticed all of the expensive cars in the parking lot. Kayse and I walked into the club and it was all that and more. You could tell the people were about something. They all looked like they were going places in life and always thinking about what their next move would be. We wanted to be around movers and shakers; thinkers.

As soon as we sat down a waiter came over to our table and asked what we wanted to drink. We ordered. When we went for our purses we were informed our tab would be taken care of by the tall gentleman in the cream suit standing by the DJ booth. Kayse and I looked at each other smiled and laughed and smiled and laughed some more. We asked the waiter to tell him thank you. We tried to find out a little about him but the waiter had never seen him in the club before. He never came over to introduce himself. When I walked in the direction he was standing, he headed out the door. He didn't return for a half hour or so. Yes, I was peeping his every move. After we finished our second drink Kayse and I looked around for the tall guy but didn't see him anywhere in site. We agreed not to accept any drinks from the tall guy. He seemed strange. Anyway, we were lightweights. We could only handle two to three drinks. Kayse and I figured we would just pay for the two drinks. We were loaded. Kayse's cousin hooked us up with the tax returns. Uncle Sam had been good to us.

The men and women in the club were really nice. Everyone seemed sure and confident in him/herself. If a guy came over from a table occupied mostly by women and asked you to dance there didn't seem to be a problem. We were among some of the most beautiful, polished looking women and men I had ever seen. Their hair, nails, shoes, and clothes were perfect. They were adorned with some of the finest jewelry, and smelled of expensive colognes and perfumes. We were really enjoying ourselves but things seemed almost too perfect.

We went to the restroom, which was done up so that there were vanities along both sides of a long hallway before you entered the toilet and sink area. Kayse and I were sitting next to each other in the vanity room when we finally figured out what was going on. The situation we had gotten ourselves into was clearly unfolding right before our eyes. A group of women were talking in the vanity area. We heard them say, "Are you going to the party in Tahoe?" "Who's sponsoring the trip and what's the cut?", "How much did you make on the last trip?", and the clincher "I know I'm not going back to Denver, way too many freaky requests there."

Who would have thought we were sitting in a club full of high-class ho's, oh sorry, call girls, escorts, whatever. You could have bought both of us for a penny that night. We didn't have any real proof but that's what it sounded like. We gathered our things and hurried toward the exit. All I could think was 'Oh my god. We have to get out of here before someone sees us.' As we were making our way to the car, the tall guy with the cream suit came out right behind us. He was yelling, "Hey wait up. Wait up."

We made it to the car and stopped. The tall guy came over with another guy about an inch taller than him. They looked alike. They had to be brothers. The cream suit guy said, "Hi my name is John and this is my brother Patrick." I said, "Hello and thank you again for the drinks even though you were no where to be found and we ended up paying for them ourselves." Just as I was getting ready to open the car door, John said, "Are you hungry? Maybe we can all go to breakfast?" Before I could say no thank you, Kayse said, "Sure. Let's go." She was looking googlely-eyed at Patrick. Then she said, "Patrick, you gotta car? I'll ride with you." O.K. Kayse had lost her mind. We never split up with total strangers. I wondered if someone slipped something in her drink? She insisted so I said ok and Kayse got in the car with Patrick. John then proceeded to get in the car with me. Oh no, I was not having it. They would all be in Patrick's car. I figured if something happened, I could call for help. Kayse was mad at me but I didn't care. Kayse got out of the car with Patrick and we met them at the twenty-four hour diner.

John and Patrick seemed to be very nice guys but they kept looking at each other like something was weighing heavily on their minds. Kayse noticed it too. I think it hit both of us at the same time. They thought we were call girls because we were at the party. This partly explained John's strange behavior at the club.

Kayse and I thought it was funny. Although we looked good, we definitely didn't measure up with our sale's outfits, knock off Swarovski-looking crystals and cubic zirconia. We were excellent imitations but we couldn't hang with the big dogs. Almost simultaneously Kayse and I said, "Excuse us, we'll be right back." We went in the restaurants small restroom and burst out into laughter. What a night!!

We returned to the table and, in unison, said, "No, we are not call girls." We all laughed and they seemed relieved. We asked John and Patrick why they were at the club. They said they were visiting from Texas. They told us they grew up around the corner from the club and their mother and sister still lived in the area. When they were younger there was another nightclub in the same spot. They thought they would check out the renovation. I asked John why he offered to buy our drinks all night and then not even introduce himself. He replied, "You and Kayse looked different than the rest of the people there. You had honest faces and since I was there, I had to fit in so I took a chance on you two. Thank you for not drinking my whole paycheck." I replied, "Right, you mean none of your paycheck." We all laughed and John picked up the check for breakfast.

We exchanged contact information. We decided to meet at the club the following week. John told us the party we walked in on was a special event and not the regular crowd. We liked the club and thought we'd give it another shot. Over the next couple of months John and Patrick met us regularly at the club. They drove from Texas every other weekend. We always had a good time. Kayse and I never had to pay for anything. They seemed real cool. They weren't pressuring us for sex. Although they denied any monogamous relationships, we didn't believe them and thought they probably had girlfriends at home. Around the third month of us knowing each other, John and Patrick asked if we would come to Texas to a birthday party they were giving for their younger brother. We thought it would be fun and we could check out the other women situation.

On the ride there we fantasized about how cool it would be if I married John and Kayse married Patrick. We thought how wonderful it would be to raise our children together. Best friends married to brothers. We would be sister-in-laws and aunt to each other's children. We could move to Texas. We could buy homes next door to each other. We had graduated in the same field so we could even work together. Perfect!

We finally arrived at the address they gave. The area didn't look clean at all. I don't think I had ever heard of Galveston at that point. The hall was actually a VFW hall. We had driven over five hundred miles so we had to go in. We were way overdressed. John and Patrick were of course the gentlemen they always were. They grabbed our hands and showed us to a table reserved for us. They brought I don't know how many people over to introduce. We felt like royalty. There was even a younger cousin who kept coming back and forth to let us know he was keeping an eye on our car so not to worry and to enjoy ourselves. The night kept getting better and better. John and his brothers, father, and uncles were Masons. They did some kind of presentation. After the presentation, a theater company gave an absolutely hilarious performance. The food was fabulous and the music was off the chain. I don't think we had partied like that since our college years. Everyone was so nice. We left when the party was over.

John and Patrick made hotel reservations before we arrived. We thought they would have reserved one room for Kayse and me. Nope. Two rooms - one for John and me and the other for Kayse and Patrick. When Kayse saw this she started laughing and singing, "Hey let's get the party started." I, on the other hand, wasn't attracted to John sexually although I really liked him. The fantasizing in the car on the way down was just talk. To this day I don't know why. The man was handsome, tall, and just out right fine. He was definitely a head turner. Well, he begged for hours. We got to the hotel around 1:00 a.m. At 4:45 a.m., he was still pleading his case. He was going on and on about what he could do to me and how I would have to keep

coming back for more like a crack head. You
know the type. I was exhausted. He wore me
down by 5:30 a.m. I said okay. At this point I
would have done almost anything to shut him
up. I wanted sleep. But before I went to sleep I
wanted to see what John had that would make
me beg for it.

We kissed. It was good. I was waking up.
He was making all the right moves. I was hot as
a firecracker. My caramel skin against his
turned me on. I never realized how well
endowed he was. I must have been out of my
mind making the man wait like that. Why would
I punish myself? Then it happened. What?
Wait? Yes, it was all of two seconds. I was
pissed. I always believed in being truthful in the
bedroom. I pushed his shoulders up so I could
look in his face. I said, "Did you?" He replied,
"I'm so sorry. I was too excited." Sorry or not I
just had to say it. "I know you didn't beg for five
hours and talk all that shit and you the one
minute brother. Not even one minute. Get the
hell off me." I turned over and went to sleep.

We were leaving that afternoon. When I
finally woke up, Kayse, John and Patrick were
already dressed, watching television and talking
about the party. John and Patrick left the hotel
while I got dressed. I told Kayse about my
disappointing morning. Kayse told me she and
Patrick decided to do something else. I asked
her what they did. Kayse told me they got high.
She hadn't slept at all. Kayse and I hadn't

smoked marijuana since college but I knew it didn't make you want to stay up all night. I asked her what kind of drugs. She replied, "We had cocaine. We snorted some and freebased the other." I felt like I was going to pass out but I didn't want Kayse to think I was a prude so I kept it together. Hell in college I smoked up more than my share of marijuana and so did Kayse. But cocaine, freebase, I was shocked. I asked her if this was a one-time thing or had they been doing it all the time. She replied, "We've snorted a little coke before when Patrick came to visit without John." I thought, 'wait; hold up. Came to visit without John?' I had to wake all the way up. Just when we were getting into the when, where, and how, the guys made it back to the room. We agreed to finish the conversation on the way home. I showered and got dressed.

Patrick and John had flowers, shrimp baskets, soda, juice and coffee. We ate, talked about the party, and packed everything up. We put everything in the car. I noticed a gift on the drivers' seat. I asked John, "Who's that for?" He said, "You. I had to do something after this morning so you would see me again." We both laughed. I enjoyed being around John. There wasn't a question of whether I would see him again. John had never expressed he was looking for something serious. I definitely wasn't looking for a serious relationship either. If things could remain the way they were, I was cool with that.

John asked me to wait until I got home to open the gift alone. I said, "O.K."

On the way home, Kayse and I talked about one thing only - her quick and sudden interest in cocaine. She thought I was overreacting because I kept going on and on about how it was habit forming and bringing up examples of people we knew growing up whose lives had been ruined because of cocaine. She waived her hand in the air at me and said, "Stop tripping Ms. Goody Two Shoes. I don't have a problem." I dropped it but deep down I didn't believe her and I didn't agree with what she was doing.

When I got home I opened the gift. It was a beautiful calfskin, red leather jacket. It was so soft. I was totally surprised. Man he must have really felt bad. I called John to thank him for the gift. I didn't think he could afford the gift so I came out and asked. I said, "John, it's beautiful. I can't accept this. I know you can't afford this." He said, "That's rude. Don't look a gift horse in the mouth. Just say thank you. Now my question to you is are we o.k?" I replied, "Thank you for the jacket. I love it. And, yes, we're great."

I hadn't talked to John or Kayse for a few weeks. Kayse had left a couple of messages on my answering machine telling me Patrick was in town. I guess it was strange that we weren't in constant communication as usual but I hardly noticed because I was busy helping my aunt prepare for our family reunion. When I finally heard from John, he told me he was moving back home and had a couple of very important things he wanted to talk about. He asked if he could come by my apartment on Saturday. I told him I would be at my family reunion cookout. I let him know he could go with me and talk there or we could wait until the following week. He said it couldn't wait and he'd see me bright and early Saturday morning.

When John arrived at my apartment he was looking very serious. Before I could invite him in good he started talking. "Look you need to talk to your girl. I think she's getting a little too deep into the drug scene. Patrick's in rehab again. My parents are blaming me for Patrick's slip." I threw my hands up and said very loudly, "Wait. Whoa. What the hell you talking about? Slow down. Kayse is deep in what drug scene? Patrick in rehab again – never knew about the first time. Why are your parents blaming you?" Everything was pouring out of him. I was trying to take it all in but it was too much. I couldn't wait until we got to the cookout so I could find Uncle Cheeks to get a strong drink and a long pull off his joint.

O.K. this was it in a nutshell. John and Patrick held 9 to 5's. Their salaries allowed them to live comfortably paycheck-to-paycheck if nothing unexpected happened, like their cars breaking down. John sold drugs. Patrick called himself a drug dealer but he used more than he sold. Patrick and Kayse started using crack and were now strung out. John had drug houses in three different states and several people working for him. When we all first met, John and Patrick were at the club making connections and deals. Patrick had always been the favored son in the family. John and Patrick did not have the same mother. Patrick's mother raised her husband's illegitimate son, John. She never let John forget it. John and Patrick's father left when they were teenagers. Patrick's mother blamed John for anything that went wrong with Patrick. The whole situation was a bunch of mess.

I wasn't thinking about anything but Kayse. The next day I called her, went by her apartment, and her mother's house. She wasn't at either place. On Monday, I went by her job on my lunch break. I found out she hadn't been to work in weeks. After I pulled out of the parking lot, I headed back to Kayse's mother's house. When I arrived, Kayse was on the phone. Kayse's mom handed me the phone. I said, "Kayse what's going on? I talked to John. I need to see you so I can see that you're o.k." Kayse replied, "It's o.k. I'm in another state in a drug rehabilitation center. John found me on Saturday, brought me here and checked me in. He's a good man. I don't know what I was thinking. I'm much better now. I'm not supposed use the phone. I begged my counselor to let me call home. I was hoping you would be at my mom's but if you weren't I had already decided I would try to sneak in a call to you. I have to go but I'll call you when I get privileges. Bye. Talk to you soon." And just like that she was gone. I felt so much better after hearing her voice. I could tell she was going to be all right.

John called frequently but things weren't the same. I looked at him differently. I would ask him, "Why do you sell drugs? Are the chances you're taking worth your freedom? Why not go back to school? What if you get arrested and lose your job? What if someone shoots you? Why do you think there's an easy way out? He would most times simply reply, "Girl please, I gotta get paid." The last time I asked him he replied, "Look at you. You're twenty-three with a bachelors and masters degree and working as a hostess at a restaurant. Your girl has a bachelors and working in a department store. Like I said, I gotta get paid." I was so insulted. Hey it was the eighties. There was a recession, Reaganomics, and the trickledown theory. There was some truth to what he was saying but it made me mad as hell. All of my life I had been told to get an education. No one could take my education away. I would always be employable. It sure didn't feel like it at the time. I was already feeling bad about where my life seemed to be going and definitely didn't want to hear my failure summed up in a couple of sentences by a drug dealing fool. I was employable and broke as hell. To make matters even worst the next week I was let go from my little hostess job.

I was putting in applications everywhere I could think of. I started to get a little depressed. Shortly after losing my job, John was laid off. He started calling all the time. Sometimes three and four times a day. I eventually started hanging out with John every day, all day. He made the move to his mother's house until he found a place of his own. We started going to fill out job applications together. He didn't really care if he got a job or not. He wasn't serious and received three job offers. He turned them down. The pay was too low. I was serious but no one was calling. My savings was running out. I wasn't going to be able to keep my apartment if I didn't get a job soon. Things were getting desperate. John suggested we get a place together. We agreed our living situation would be temporary, just until I could get back on my feet. We found a really nice place. There were two bedrooms. We agreed to have separate bedrooms. John and I had not been intimate since the first time. Yeah we kissed and hugged but no sexual intercourse. To tell the truth I was always guarded with him. I never opened up to him. Especially after finding out what he really did to make money.

I moved in my bedroom furniture and we went shopping for everything else. John really didn't have anything and he didn't care for my furniture because he thought it was too feminine. As long as he was buying my feeling was whatever. When John and I went shopping

I experienced something I had never experienced
before. For the first time in my life I felt a true
sense of buying power. It was freeing. The store
did not have price tags on any of its pieces. We
went in the store and looked at things we
wanted. We bought whatever we thought we
needed without the constraint of being able to
afford it. I picked out the living and dining room
furniture and custom blinds for the windows
throughout the apartment. I heard John
negotiating the price of two nightstand lamps
with the salesman. They finally settled on five
hundred dollars each. I had never purchased
anything without having to be concerned with
the price. The experience gave me such a good
feeling. It was intoxicating. I wanted to feel it
over and over again.

The next week there was a party we both
wanted to go to. John was going to get a new
suit and asked if I would help him pick
something out. It wasn't like I was busy so I
went along. I kept looking at a coral silk dress.
It was so pretty. I didn't have the money to buy
it. John surprised me by buying it for me. We
went out that night - him with his nice navy suit
and me with my beautiful coral silk dress. While
we were at the club we took a picture. John was
sitting down, I was standing kind of to the side
but in front of him and he had his arm around
my waist with I don't know how many hundreds
fanned out in his free hand. Yes, ghetto
fabulous. I could feel myself getting caught up

in his lifestyle. I couldn't fight against it. I didn't want to.

The next thing I knew I was rolling with John to different states checking on his drug houses. The drug houses were a trip. Nothing like I had ever seen. People lived there and the houses were actually presentable and clean. John wouldn't have it any other way. There were people from all walks of life. Some had hard lives but the majority of them had normal lives before they sacrificed everything for a high. You haven't seen anything until you've seen a woman who held the title for the most beautiful woman in the state getting high on crack. I saw how paranoid the drugs made her. For well over an hour, she rubbed her index finger back and forth through the carpet to make sure she got every crumb of the crack rock she thought had fallen. Nothing fell. It was a sad thing to see. Oh and the arguments that started over drugs between supposed friends were never ending. I saw too many arguments to count begin because someone took too long of a pull off of the pipe. After a couple of trips, I often thought 'Damn, where am I? And what am I doing?'

John and I got closer and closer and eventually we were in the same bedroom. I was at the beauty shop or the mall all the time. My car note, our rent and our utilities were paid ahead of time. I didn't really want for anything but I wasn't happy. There was nothing really deep about our relationship. Cuddling, hugging, taking long walks in the park, watching the sunset, going to a movie or to the theater were out of the question. These things defied all logic for John. Time was money and everything else was bullshit. If it didn't make money, John didn't understand it. All of our conversations were centered on how to make money. No matter the subject, it always ended with making more money.

I was always nervous John was going to get arrested and I would have to testify against him. From the beginning, I told him I was going to sing like a canary if he got caught. I meant it. I was going to tell everything and anything I knew. He thought it was hilarious and would say "Girl you don't know anything."

I was drinking Pepto-Bismol extra strength like water. I kept a large bottle in the bottom of my huge Louis Vuitton purse. I wasn't just paranoid either. John's beeper constantly went off. He received threats all the time and we were once in a high-speed car chase. It was scary as hell. Drug dealers that wanted to take over John's drug territory followed us in a car from one of John's drug houses. They drove up close behind us and hit our car from behind. John sped up and they began to chase us. John was driving with one hand on the steering wheel and holding on to a gun under his seat with his other hand. He yelled at me to "Get down." Somehow John lost them. From that day on, I never went to his drug houses or anywhere near them.

Eventually, we started to drift apart. Our superficial relationship was slowly fading away and what was left was the reality that we had nothing substantial between us. We had furnished an entire apartment, bought jewelry, clothes, shoes, purses, paid rent, car notes, etc. I felt it was time to stop. We had been lucky and enough was enough. I started looking for a job again and found something in my field within two weeks of looking. I started going to a small church in the neighborhood. I thought about the past five months and thanked God he had seen me through and asked it be put on John's heart to leave the drug game alone. John went to church with me a few times before he decided to join. I was very happy. I loved John as a person and wanted him to be safe.

A short while later, John told me he was going to get out of the business. If he planned everything just right, he figured it would take him about a month to get totally out. He was going to step out and let his partner take over everything. Of course, nothing went right. Things went horribly. John left on a Thursday and was to return early Saturday morning. Late Thursday evening there was a knock at the door. I looked through the peephole and there was Jake and Carl from a house in Tennessee. I opened the door and said, "Hey, what ya'll doing here? Come on in." I noticed they were covered

in a red colored paint. I asked, "What you all
been doing? Ya'll been painting? Here I'm
getting some water. Ya'll want some water or we
have some juice, pop..." Jake cut me off and
said, "Look we really like you. You're cool but
we had to fuck your boy up. All we want to
know is where the drugs are?" I replied, "I don't
know about no drugs. Look anywhere you want
to. What did you do to John?" Carl replied, "We
cut him up. That's what's on our shirts, his
blood." I said, "Why did you do that? Where is
he?" Jake said, "Ain't no drugs here. Let's go.
We left him in the house." Surprisingly, I was
very calm. As Jake and Carl were running out
of the apartment, I was calling Patrick to tell him
what was going on. I had to call for a ride. I
wasn't going to go anywhere by myself. John
had driven my car because it needed new tires
and he was going to get them for me on his way
home. Now Jake and Carl had my car. Patrick
had left rehab and was the only one I could call.

It seemed as though Patrick got to our
place in two minutes. I looked out the window
and there had to be twenty police cars outside. I
just knew they were there for Carl and Jake.
You wouldn't believe it but the police were
arresting another drug dealer that lived in
another one of the complex's buildings. Patrick
was looking real crazy and nervous when he
came into the apartment. We left.

Patrick and I made it to the dope house.
The living room was torn apart. The glass table

was smashed to the ground. They had actually stabbed John with a huge piece of the broken glass from the table. Someone called the police and John was rushed to a nearby hospital. When Patrick and I arrived at the hospital John's family was in an uproar because he would not go into surgery until he saw me. Oh my God they hated me from that point on. They already thought John was doing too much for me and not giving them enough. John pulled me down to him, hugged me and whispered, "I've been bullshitting all the time. I love you. Be here when I wake up." I said, "I love you too. See you when you come out of surgery." What else was I going to say, the man was in critical condition.

John suffered a couple of broken ribs, internal bleeding and a punctured lung. He stayed in the hospital for a couple of weeks. While he was in the hospital I decided to go to a house party given by some of my college friends. We got really drunk, played bid whist, and talked about old times. We had run out of clear liquor so some of us decided to go to the store before it closed. As we were driving down the street I saw a car that looked just like mine. I said, "Stop. That's my car." Everyone in the car knew about John and what had just happened. They started laughing and saying I was trippin'. I insisted we stop. I got out of the car and opened the car door with my key. No one could believe it. Carl and Jake had left the car locked and in a relatively safe place. I couldn't believe it.

While I was driving, someone suggested I call the police so they could stop looking for my car. I called the police. They informed me I had to bring the car to the police station immediately. If I were caught driving the car I would be arrested for theft of a motor vehicle and filing a fraudulent insurance claim. Imagine this, five very drunk people in a police station trying to explain how we came across the car. I think the police just wanted us to go away. We were so paranoid. We thought the police were going to wait until we drove off and arrest us for drunk driving so we told Jackie, the most sober, to drive. We made it back to the party and resumed activities as if nothing had ever happened.

On the day of John's release, the doctor told him he needed to make sure he used the breathing machine they gave him two to three times a day and to make sure he remained active. For some reason John equated this to increased sexual activity. While he was thinking of new sexual positions, I was making up my mind to leave John as soon as he could breathe on his own.

During John's recuperation period, he started attending church and bible study regularly. I was glad to see he was progressing both physically and spiritually. He had gotten so into the Bible that he told the study group they could meet at our apartment. At first I didn't mind but it soon became apparent John was using the Bible to critique my every move. He pissed me off on a daily basis. Everyday he tried to beat me up with one bible scripture or another.

Approximately two months later I was back home with my parents. John tried everything in the book to get me to come back. He would show up everywhere. He would come by my parent's house, sit by me in church, come by my job, and even once came into the beauty shop when I was getting my hair done. I continually told John we were not going to get back together. I even found another church to attend. The last straw was when I let John convince me to meet him at the church we started attending together. I thought this would be a good thing. I was comfortable there and maybe John and I could be friends. Wrong.

I went to church and there he was sitting with his ex-girlfriend. I could not believe he would use the church as a place to try to humiliate and hurt me. To top things off the sermon was about relationships, trust, and commitment. I couldn't really focus on the message because I was too busy praying to God that He forgive me for all of the cuss words I was calling John in my head. After the service was over, there was a beeline of women darting towards me. Each of them gave me some form of condolence for losing my man and offered their support. It took everything I had to hold back from cussing those no man having, didn't know what the hell they were talking about women from heaven to hell and back again. By the time I made it to the door, John was standing there with a big devilish smile on his face. I smiled back and said "God bless you my brother" and walked away. I was done.

I started a new job with the city a few months later and moved to a new apartment. I put John and the whole experience behind me. About a year later, after John stop making unexpected visits to my apartment, I saw him on TV with a well-known politician. He worked that for a while. Today John is a minister with the same I gotta get paid attitude cloaked in nicer words. He tailored his game for a different venue. He's now dealing in the name of the Lord. He is who he is. He's not married. He calls every now and then to say hello and brag about the material things he has acquired. Kayse never returned home. She moved to Colorado. Patrick joined her about a year later. They married and never looked back. They have a beautiful home, two children and one grandchild. John and Patrick rarely speak.

Insight
The question was how did I get here? It was a lot of things but most of all it was being young and stupid. There are women sitting in prison today for being in the wrong place at the

wrong time or with the wrong person. It was anger. I followed the formula of education equals success. I worked hard. I spent a lot of time and money yet success seemed so far out of reach. It was disappointment. I had both Bachelor and Master of Science degrees but I was the working poor. I was barely making it on the meager earnings from my hostess job and soon lost that income. I had high hopes. I believed what my parents told me. I believed what society told me. But in reality, I was doing no better than my high school peers who had not gone to college. I allowed my circumstances to guide my decisions and in many case's my non-decisions.

In life, nothing worth having comes free. There's always a price. No matter how big or small. John wanted the quick and easy way. I now know for sure such a path does not exist. Money was the driving force that pushed John to take chances with his life and freedom. He was willing to do whatever it took to get money, power and control. I often think about the risks I took and the vulnerable position I put myself in. I was reaping the benefits and secretly enjoying the ride even though deep down inside I knew it was wrong. The money, clothes, clubs, and excitement were all very appealing and like I said intoxicating. No matter how twisted it sounds, there was an appeal that fed my curiosity. Being with John was a rush and somewhere deep inside I liked it no matter how much I would like to say today I didn't.

John was a strong man. He wasn't afraid of anything. He made me feel safe in his presence. He was a hustler. There was something so sexy about the way he could make a way out of no way. He was a thinker, confident and reliable. His word was his bond. If he said he was going to do something you didn't ever have to worry about it getting done. How it got done was another story. John was the type of man that couldn't take no for an answer. He would crash and burn first. Unfortunately, the collateral damage caused by his actions would, in most cases, leave a trail of destruction.

With all of John's positive attributes, I believe he will always make a way to live in this world and most will never ever peep his hand of deception. His relentless drive to acquire money and material things doesn't allow him to feel or care deeply about anything or anyone. Don't get me wrong. He was never mean to me but passion and affection were emotions that escaped him. He saw things he wanted and did whatever it took to get them, including people. I think he cared as much as he could. I thank God I was able to walk away, to start again, to take seriously my freedom, to realize there are no successes without work and to respect and love me first. There are many who can't pray this prayer. I know I was spared. For that gift, I am thankful.

RITA

Jason - The For Appearances Sake Man

    Jason graduated from college, worked a nine to five, and was very involved with his fraternity and community. He drives a Cadillac and always dresses to impress. He's about 5'9 and average looking. I met Jason about four months after I left John. We had just been hired by the city. We were two of seven new minority hire's resulting from a lawsuit that found the city had intentionally not hired qualified minority candidates for city jobs. I was not attracted to Jason at all. He seemed nice enough but he was definitely not my type and besides dating someone at work was asking for trouble.

    We were partnered during training and went out after work for drinks two to three times a week with the other trainees. During this time I got to know Jason and the other trainees a lot better. Strangely enough Jason and I were really the only available single people in the whole class. The others were either married, engaged, living with someone, had baby mamas and daddies, or were gay. We were almost pushed together. We could stay out all night, go where we wanted, do what we wanted, and had no one to answer to. Jason was really a cool guy. I still wasn't physically attracted to him but I enjoyed being around Jason. He made me laugh. And what was so cute about it was that it was if he had practiced what he would say to make sure I laughed every day.

Eventually, Jason and I went from hanging out during the week to hanging out on weekends too. A couple of months after we had finished the training session for work, I moved to a new apartment. I was so happy to leave my parent's house again and move to my own place. I had mentioned I was moving to my colleagues. A couple of the guys offered to help me move. I didn't have a lot of things but I could use the help. It worked out perfectly, as one was leaving another was coming to help. Jason was the last one to come. He helped me finish getting things in order and came by the next day to see if I needed anything or if there was anything else he could do. As time went on we became closer and closer. I met his friends and family and he met mine. We were friends, nothing more than good friends.

My ex-boyfriend, John would come around every now and then for a number of reasons. I was so upset he found out where I lived. To this day, I don't know who told him. Anyway, he would find some small trinket, necklace, piece of clothing, or anything to come by to return it to me.   He would then begin his long drawn out apology for the church incident and make a plea as to why we should get back together.   It was tiring and no matter how forceful or often I said "I accept your apology" and "no, we can't get back together", he would find his way back at my door with some little piece of something returning it, apologizing and pleading.

One Saturday afternoon, John was at my apartment. He told me he had accepted the fact that we were over and just wanted to be friends. He began to tell me about his new relationship. All I could think was good, good, good. While we were talking my doorbell rang and then there was a quick knock on the door.   I didn't even have time to get to the intercom to ask who it was or buzz the person up. I looked through the peephole and it was Jason standing there with a six-pack of Mike's Hard Lemonade. I opened the door and Jason came in.   He looked shocked and in awe to see John sitting on the sofa in the living room.   John stood up and towered over Jason.   John reached out his hand and said, "What's up man?"   Jason shook John's hand and replied, "It's all good."

Jason said, "I see you have company so I'll talk to you later. Here I bought you this." As Jason was handing me the Lemonade, John burst into laughter and said, "Man the next time you bring this lady something you need to step your game up and not bring that bullshit."   I quickly moved Jason to the door and said, "I'll talk to you later." Jason left. I put John out of my apartment, cleaned up and called Jason a couple hours later. When I called, Jason didn't pick up so I left him a message. He called me back about two hours later. By this time I had rented a couple of movies and was very content with just chilling by myself. During our phone conversation Jason was very short and distant. You could tell he was irritated. You could feel it in his responses. I asked him was there anything wrong but he insisted there wasn't. I said, "O.k." and we hung up.

Now I was no fool. I knew exactly what was wrong with Jason. I knew Jason was interested in me and I knew he was pissed because John was at my place and he didn't know what that meant. Over the next couple of weeks Jason and I were just co-workers. We didn't go out to lunch or have drinks after work together. I asked him to go out with me several times but he refused by making up some prior engagement excuse. I was really sad about it because I felt I was responsible for destroying a good friendship and hurting Jason's feelings. I thought if I just let him get things in order in his mind then everything would work itself out. I thought he needed space and maybe I did too. I really missed being around him though. More than I would have anticipated I would.

Early on a Saturday morning my phone rang. It was Jason. He asked if I wanted to go to breakfast. I was so happy to hear from him I said, "Of course. What time?" He said, "Can you be ready in about thirty minutes?" I replied, "I'll be downstairs waiting." When I got in the car there was a real eerie solemn feeling in the air. I asked Jason what was wrong and he replied, "Can I have hug?" It felt really strange. Had someone died? Was someone ill? I didn't know what was going on? I hugged him and he held on really tight. When we released each other Jason smiled and the eerie strange feeling was gone. Jason was his old self. I asked again if there was something wrong and he just laughed and said, "Nope. All good." It was eight o'clock in the morning and I wasn't a morning person so enough with the inquisition. I was hungry. We went to IHOP. We talked and laughed and talked and laughed. I asked Jason why he stopped coming around and if it had anything to do with John. He said, "Let's wait until we get out of here for that conversation." I agreed. Before we could get to the car I was reminding Jason about the much-needed conversation we postponed until we left the restaurant.

When we got in the car, Jason started talking about how he wished he could just go somewhere for peace of mind. I was really feeling that so I said, "Me too. Let's just ride. When we get tired we'll stop." Jason immediately got excited. He started checking balances on credit cards and calling his boys to let them know he wouldn't be hanging with them. He even called his mother to let her know he might be in very late or early in the morning and not to worry. Then I got excited. I called to check my balance at the bank. Hell, I always knew what I had available on the credit cards, nothing. We gassed up and hit the highway. The spontaneity of it all was exhilarating and so freeing. I loved it. We talked about the awkwardness of the day he came over and John was at my apartment; how it made him feel like a chump; how he felt I should have told John to leave especially after making the comment about the lemonade; how he really wanted to have a serious relationship with me; how he thought we were on the same page and could achieve a lot together; how he knew I really cared about him too but I wouldn't let it touch me; and how he would spend the rest of his life just trying to make me happy. I was blown away. I knew he liked me but I didn't know it was this deep. I could only reply, "Whew, that's a lot to think about." Spending the rest of our lives together? We hadn't been on a real date yet. I wondered how he could know all of this in such a short time. We agreed to give it a rest and pick it up later. We turned the music up and kept cruising to Smokey Robinson.

We made a few stops. We stopped and checked out whatever looked interesting along the way. We were having fun. We stopped at a rest area with a swing set, monkey bars, and a huge slide. We played on the equipment and sat and talked more on the swings. We talked until dusk. I started turning things over in my mind.

Now here was a good man who saying he was willing to do whatever it took to make me happy. O.K., I wasn't physically attracted to him but he had great potential. Who did I think I was? This is what men meant when they said women say they want a good man but when one presents himself we push them away and go for the bad boy every time. I had just been in a relationship with a real bad boy and here was this decent guy who was interested and I wasn't giving him the time of day. I was just playing with him. I mean really, I wasn't attracted to John at first either and he was fine. Was it all about looks or could someone grow on you? It seemed logical a person could look better and better if he was treating you like a queen. What the hell? If it didn't work I could always say that. Maybe I would give it a try. I liked being around him. He seemed to really care about me. I had to think more about it but I was leaning towards giving us a try.

It was getting later and later and we were about three hours away from home. I suggested we stop at a hotel and start fresh in the morning. Jason replied, "Yeah but there's only going to be one room." I replied, "That's fine." He was charged. He was like a kid in a candy store whose parents just told him to have his fill. We got the room, ordered room service, watched a movie, and fell asleep in our clothes. It was all rather romantic. The next morning Jason got up early, showered and went to wash and gas the car. While I was waiting for him to return I did a lot of soul searching. When he returned he apologized for taking such a long time. He couldn't find a car wash.

We left the hotel, stopped at Cracker Barrel and prepared ourselves for the three-hour ride back home. When we got in the car, I blurted out, "O.K. Let's try it, me and you." When I think back on it all, I realize I had to blurt it out otherwise I would have never brought myself to say it. I wasn't feeling real sure. I was almost forcing it. Hell, I WAS forcing it.

Well we started dating and it was absolute bliss. It was the little things like a rose or flower on my car windshield, a love note hiding somewhere unexpected, cute and thoughtful gifts, being considerate, not smothering at all. He had his friends and I had mine. We all did things together and separately. The sex was awesome. He worked really hard to please me. I often thought about what I would have passed up looking only at the superficial aspects of a person. As time went on we got closer.

We decided to move in together. I had to put my foot down. He was still staying with his mother, saving his money, and gradually taking over my bottom chest drawer. We bought a house and got married one year later. Our wedding was a beautiful and exquisite affair. I loved him with everything I had in me. The first year of our marriage we traveled a lot and were truly still in the honeymoon phase. The next six months was an emotional roller coaster ride that took its toll on our relationship. We found out we were pregnant, which we were ecstatic about, and that his mother had cancer, which kept us in a sort of panic-stricken mode. I was close to his mother. I loved his mother. She was a wonderful woman. She was supportive of our marriage from the very beginning. She was so excited about becoming a grandmother. When our daughter, Destiny, was born she cried uncontrollably because she thought she wouldn't live to see her grandchild. My parents, on the other hand, always thought I could do better, especially my mother. What mother doesn't?

It was almost exactly at the two-year mark that things began to go wrong. We were at one of his high school friend's house for a party. I was walking around the house looking for Jason. I came to room where the door was barely cracked. I saw the back of Jason's head. I opened the door and there they were. Jason and about seven of his friends were snorting cocaine. I couldn't believe it. How is it I never knew he did drugs? I just looked at him, walked out of the room and went back to the party. Shortly after, Jason found me downstairs in the game room shooting pool. He acted as if nothing was wrong. He acted like it was everyday a woman finds out her husband does drugs. I thought if that's how he wanted to play it fine. But we were definitely talking about it first thing in the morning. I wanted to make sure he was sober for the much needed conversation.

Early the next morning I woke Jason up so we could talk. We got up. We had hot tea, bagels, cream cheese and a couple pieces of bacon. I asked Jason when he started doing drugs. He laughed and said, "Girl, please. You know I told you when we first met I like to do a little coke sometimes." O.K. now I was pissed. He has just insulted my intelligence and tried to play me like a damn fool. Now up until this point I had never even raised my voice or cursed Jason. Not that he hadn't heard me do either it was just it had never been directed at him. I replied, "Wait a damn minute. I know the fuck you ain't trying to insinuate you told me that you are a damn dope head and I just forgot. Motherfucker, when you met me I was with the dope man. What the hell kind of sense would that make? I'ma leave the dope man for the dope fiend. You need to come again with that bullshit. Now, I'm asking again. What the fuck is up?"

Jason looked puzzled. He became very apologetic and assured me this was something he did on occasion. I replied, "Okay, good. Since it's only on occasion it shouldn't bother you to never do it again." Jason's response was "It's not that serious. I don't ever have to do it.

You're making a mountain out of a molehill." In my mind the whole drug situation was over but the reality was it was at the root of all that would become wrong in our marriage.

As we were approaching the third year of marriage it was quite noticeable Jason was doing drugs frequently. I didn't help the situation because at this point Jason disgusted me. I asked Jason for a divorce. He pleaded and begged me to reconsider. We agreed to give it another six months. The next six months were absolutely wonderful. He told me he even stopped hanging out with his friends that were known drug users. Although he would not get professional help, I could see he was making an effort. He didn't trust the referral through the job's addiction program would be confidential. I wanted him to get professional help but understood his reluctance to some extent. Adherence to the confidentiality rules by workers at our job's addiction program was questionable at best. We all knew or heard about colleagues who were in the program through the rumor mill at work. He was doing great so I decided to be the "good wife" and stand by my man. He was keeping his word, right?

I was really happy during this time. We were always entertaining. We had parties and cookouts at our house all the time. Our friends and family constantly complemented us on our accomplishments. We were seen as the perfect couple with the perfect child and perfect home.

Something Jason lived for. He would strut around with his chest poked out and his head held high. Things seemed to be getting back to like they were when we were first married. Even though things seemed to be getting back on the right track, I was still worried. Sometimes I would catch Jason just staring off into space. He seemed at times so very bored.

We lived on a block with older couples. They had raised their families and most were retired. I was so excited when a young family moved down the street from us. Jason went to their house and introduced himself the day they moved in. He invited them to our house. The couple and their two young children were at our door the next day. We were outside on the patio grilling so it worked out perfectly. Hank, Shirley, eight-year old Caleb and five-year old Carressa seemed like a very nice family. Hank and Jason bonded immediately. Shirley and I talked like we had known each other for years. Caleb and Carressa looked after Destiny like she was their younger sister.

Over the next year, I learned quite a bit about our new friends. Shirley had graduated from high school and completed two years of college. She worked in a factory and had a pretty good income because she had been there for years. Hank graduated from high school and worked through a temporary agency that found work for ex-felons. Hank had done time for selling drugs. He was very young when he was arrested and served eighteen months in the county lockup. It was difficult for him to find a permanent position because of his record. The permanent job he had relocated a few months into them living at their current address leaving him back at the drawing board and behind the eight ball. Shirley and Hank had met at Shirley's job. Hank was working there temporarily. They started dating and the rest is history.

Jason and Hank became close. They did everything together. Shirley and I were like sisters. We shopped together, went to the same hair stylist, got our nails and feet done together, used the same pediatrician, family doctor and gynecologist. We became so close that some of my friends resented Shirley and warned me she really wasn't a true friend. None of them had any proof of this but had a feeling something just wasn't right. I didn't pay them any attention. Hell, while they were out living the single life I was at home talking to Shirley about what brand of diapers truly kept babies drier. About a year and a half after Shirley and Hank moved to the neighborhood, Shirley and I found out we were pregnant. She was three months and I was almost two months along.

Jason and Hank were ecstatic. One day they burst into Shirley's house loud, drunk and singing an idiotic rap song they made up about keeping their wives barefoot and pregnant while waving pink and blue bubble gum cigars.

Shirley gave birth to a daughter named Cassandra. I gave birth to a son named Daniel. Soon after the birth of our son, Jason's mom died. This would begin the most hellacious time of my life. Jason didn't have to be the good boy for his mother anymore. She was gone. He took off his mask and truly showed me who he really was. Jason's drug use began again with a vengeance. At first I believed it was his way of showing and dealing with his hurt and pain after his mother's death. It wouldn't be long before I realized Jason used drugs because he wanted to. He loved drugs more than me. He loved drugs more than his children.

Jason and Hank started staying out later and later. Sometimes they wouldn't come home until the next day. Jason started lying about any and everything. He would offer lies to questions that hadn't even been asked. I gained about twenty pounds. Jason and I weren't having sex anymore. Instead of talking about diapers and babies, Shirley and I were constantly talking about how unhappy we were in our marriages. The tables turned so quickly.

Jason acted as if he was disgusted with me. Although I tried to be strong and pull on inner strength and stayed prayed up I was sad and hurt. I couldn't believe I had allowed this little ugly man to strip me of my confidence. I was overweight, my husband wouldn't touch me, I was overworked between the jobs and the kids, and I was lonely. I poured myself into my kids, work, and decided to go back to school to get my Ph.D. I think the best thing that happened was that I got back in school. I was no longer contrived to the boring conversations with Shirley about our marriages. I started to meet people that wanted the same things I wanted out of life and were taking the necessary steps to reach their goals. As time went on I became stronger. It never fails with God on your side and a carefully laid out plan you can't lose. I figured I would complete the Ph.D. program in five years and then I would get a divorce and move on. At first my friends couldn't understand why I wouldn't get divorced immediately. I told them I would stay married to Jason long enough to qualify for his pension. I did not plan to marry again and thought I should get some kind of long-term benefit. They were satisfied with this explanation and thought I was being smart. The real truth was I wanted my family, my husband and my marriage.

I tried to talk to Jason. I wanted to know if he wanted the marriage or me anymore but he was totally shut off. I felt like I was suffocating. I started having panic attacks and couldn't remember when the last time I had a peaceful night's sleep.

Shirley called me one day and told me she found out that Jason and Hank were doing drugs on the regular. As if this was a revelation. Was she for real? She was in so much denial. She also talked about her and Hank not having sex anymore. He couldn't get an erection due to the heavy drug use. This statement hit me like a ton of bricks. All of this time I was thinking Jason didn't want to have sex because I had gained weight and was disgusted by me. I remembered the few times we attempted to have sex before we stopped being intimate at all. The times he couldn't get an erection and the times he would get an erection and it wouldn't last. How could he let me think all this time it was me? This had messed with my self-esteem like nothing else. I had always been very confident. Men had always liked me. I had never had a problem attracting a man, and not just any man, a decent man. How could I have let this drug addicted liar strip me of my confidence and let myself believe I was someone other than who I knew myself to be? How could I allow him to hurt me so deeply?

I confronted Jason and all he could say was "I never said it was you." Even with all of what was going on and the pain I was feeling, I still wanted to salvage our marriage. I thought about how a divorce would impact our children and pleaded with Jason to get help with his drug addiction and to go to a marriage counselor. He refused to do either. I attempted to persuade him on several occasions thereafter. He continually denied the seriousness of his addiction and was convinced we could work our marital problems out ourselves. It got to the point whenever I brought the subject up he would get perturbed and leave the house. I was disappointed he didn't want to salvage what we had. With all of the disappointment and hurt there were days I thought I would not be able to make it another day. I look back now and realize that through it all I was getting stronger and stronger. I had a plan. It took me six years to finish my Ph.D. I told Jason I was leaving him and filing for a divorce.

I took a job in another state. My children and I moved. On the day the children and I were moving, Jason was sitting on a crate in the living room in disbelief. The movers were working right around him. I heard them outside laughing and saying, "Well, another one bites the dust." I guess they had seen this scenario numerous times before so without knowing the story they knew the deal.

When I finished packing my car up, Jason came over to me and asked, "Am I going with you?" He was so pitiful. I was so taken aback. Did this man know or realize what it had taken for me to come to this point? I replied, "Hell no. You're not going anywhere with me. I'm trying to move forward. What do you think? I'm going to take you with me and then you find the drug addicts where we're going. You're not going to embarrass me. I'm starting a new life without you. I'm not taking any of this garbage with me. But I tell you what. Get yourself together and we'll talk about it." He walked away so dejected but I couldn't think about him anymore. My children and I had a twelve-hour drive ahead of us.

Over the next six months Jason came to visit several times. He slept on the couch and seemed understanding and content just to be with his family. We talked for hours on the phone and during his visits about his drug use. Although he promised he was not using drugs, I couldn't trust what he was saying because he had stopped and started before or at least that's what he told me and that's what I believed. The kids were really pushing for me to let their dad stay with us. I started to give reconciliation some consideration but I never stopped the divorce proceedings.

Approximately four months later the truth reared its ugly head. It was during the Christmas holiday season. Jason was supposed to be en route to visit for the holidays. He called from a strange phone number and informed me his car had been towed and he would have to wait a couple of days before he could get it. No problem, I thought. Instead of two weeks, he'd be with us for a week and a half.

When he arrived I was looking for the children's Christmas gifts so I could wrap them and put them under the tree. I absolutely love Christmas so I always went overboard. I had already wrapped the gifts I had bought. Jason gave me two large plastic bags filled with gifts from the dollar store. You do what you can do until you can do better but there was no good reason, in my mind, Jason could have only purchased dollar store gifts for our children. This really bothered me because it was an indication that there was something really wrong. I asked Jason about the gifts. He told me he had to pay quite a bit of money to get his car out of the pound. It still didn't make sense. I knew how much money he made and I hadn't asked him for a dime since I had left. I decided to let it go and investigate after the holidays. The kids had strange looks on their faces when they opened the gifts. You could see they were disappointed but they just smiled and said thank you.

A couple of days after Jason returned home, I was talking to him on the phone when Shirley called. I told Jason Shirley was calling and I would call him back. He started stuttering and asking me all kinds of silly things to keep me on the phone. I clicked over to Shirley and told her to hold on. I clicked back over to Jason and told him I would call him right back because Shirley was holding. When I got back to Shirley she began to tell me about the day Jason and Hank went to jail. Apparently, the day Jason was supposed to be on his way to my house for Christmas, he and Hank were arrested in a drug house buying drugs from an undercover police officer. This explained the strange phone number, the dollar store gifts, and why he was holding me on the phone when I told him Shirley was on the other line. I was totally pissed no I was mad as hell. I got hot all over. I was raging.

I called Jason back and cussed him out so bad. He was still doing drugs. He was still lying. All of the hours of talking were filled with lies. It had been a year since I filed for divorce. The next month the divorce was final. I lost so-called friends and my reputation because of our divorce. Jason told people I got my Ph.D. and left him for no reason and some people believed him. Of course, people only saw what was presented - a nice house, nice family, and nice couple. I never talked to Shirley again. Shirley and Hank are still married. Jason and Hank are no longer friends. Jason is still lying, using drugs, and living behind his mask.

Insight

It's a damning thing to wake up one morning and realize everything you thought was real isn't. Jason was a master at hiding who he really was from everyone. So long as the outside world saw him the way he wanted to be portrayed he was happy. The portrayal of the happy family helped Jason hide from the world. In his ferocious and steadfast attempt to protect and cover up his real identity anyone close to him got used up.

I wanted my marriage and family. Jason's drug use and his commitment to his habit drove a wedge between us. The drug was what was important to him. I spent years praying, pleading and simply wishing for our situation to get better. It didn't. Jason wasn't ready to be drug free and I couldn't make him be ready. Even my leaving and taking our children hundreds of miles away didn't make Jason want to stop using drugs. He continued to lie and use drugs. He was selfish.

I remember going to church and listening to the minister. He would sometimes preach about love and support in a relationship during the good and bad times. He would say in marriage we are often tested. The tests, he said, would be difficult and sometimes we wouldn't know if we would be able to withstand the pressures. He said to always know God does not give you more than you can handle. As Jason and my relationship became more and more strained, my belief that our relationship would be healed faded.

One Sunday, I was feeling mighty low. I was depressed and felt all torn up inside. I was in church but my mind was wondering. I couldn't focus on the sermon. I began to pray a silent prayer. I asked God for help. Then I heard the minister say, "Every relationship or coming together is not ordained by God." Without consciously trying to, I stood up and left the church. For days I thought long and hard about what I had heard. Those words gave me the strength to move on. Maybe Jason and I just weren't meant to be. Could it have been just that simple? I tried for years. Once I stopped holding on to a situation, to the relationship, I was able to let go. I had done all I could do. Jason, at one time, was a good man, good husband, and good father. Without the influence of drugs maybe he could be again but I will never know. Today, that's fine with me.

CHARMAINE

Phillip - The I Like A Simple Life Man

Phillip is a mama's boy who knows how to treat a woman mostly because he was raised with all women – his grandmother, mother and three older sisters. His father left his mother before he was born for a woman down the street from where his parents lived. He vowed he would never leave his wife and children when he got married. He worked as a construction worker and seemed to really enjoy it. He graduated high school and completed two years of college. At the end of his second year in college, he realized college was not for him and set out to find out for himself what he really wanted to do. There was little resistance to him leaving school because his grandmother, mother and older sisters were there to support him in whatever decision he made. After working several jobs, Phillip began working on a construction site and found he really liked working outdoors and physical labor.

I met Phillip at a do-it-yourself car wash. It was a beautiful day and I was bored. I couldn't get in contact with any of my girlfriends so I decided to go to the car wash. A tall man in the next stall came over and asked if I had change for a dollar because the change machine didn't seem to be working. I told him to hang on a minute and I'd check my purse. We were the only two at the car wash so I got in my car and locked the doors and checked for the change.

I got out of the car and walked to the end of the stall and called out to him. I gave him the change. He said, "thank you." I went back to washing my car. Several other cars pulled into the other stalls. I felt a lot more comfortable with other people being there. Paranoid? Maybe. Safe? Definitely!

I started working on the tires and as I was bending down I could feel someone standing over me. I turned suddenly and the guy I had given the change to was standing over me. He said, "I'm so sorry I didn't mean to scare you. I just wanted to introduce myself and thank you again for the change." I said, "No problem, you're welcome." He reached out his hand to shake mine and told me his name was Phillip. As he shook my hand he took the rag I was cleaning the tires with from my other hand and said, "Let me get that." Right before he offered I was kicking myself for even going to the car wash. I had ruined a perfectly good manicure. What was I thinking? I should have gone to the automatic. I knew I didn't like washing no damn car. I said, "Thank you", he finished the job, and we said goodbye.

On my way home I thought now there's a real gentleman. I should have chatted him up a little more. Oh well. A couple of weeks passed and I thought about Phillip again. Maybe if I went to the car wash I'd run into him. He seemed to be a nice guy so he's probably involved with someone. I decided to go anyway. If he's not there I'll just go on down to the automatic.

On this particular day the car wash was packed. As soon as I turned into the stall another car pulled in behind me. It was Phillip. All kinds of thoughts about it being karma and meant to be ran through my mind. We got out of our cars. The last time Phillip was there he was washing a truck. This time he was washing car. I thought oh shoot that's probably his wife or woman's car. He immediately came over and said hello and asked, "why are you washing your own car, where's your man?" I replied, "You're getting a little personal aren't you?" He smiled and said, "I'll do it for you just don't tell your man, I don't want no drama."

We talked the whole time he was washing my car about nothing but we both managed to let each other know that we were single. When he finished washing my car he asked if I was going to leave or stay and talk while he finished. I didn't have anything else to do and besides I was really there looking for him although he didn't know that. Later I found out that he was at the carwash the week before hoping that I would be there. Oh it had to be a sign. I just knew the love gods were shining down on me.

Before we started officially dating I met his grandmother, mother and sisters. They all seemed very nice and were very talkative. There were all kinds of questions. What do you do for a living? Do you have any children? Can you cook? Etc. Of course I knew they were sizing me up and Phillip was looking for their approval. Phillip had worked hard for his modestly furnished three-bedroom home on about a half acre of land, car, truck, and nice sized savings account.

I wanted something different. I was the party girl. Unlike me, Phillip only drank beer every now and then, didn't go out to clubs, and preferred to rent DVD's and watch movies at home. He had an extensive collection of CD's and old albums and before long we were spending a lot of time together listening to music and getting to know each other. It seemed like I was over at his place all the time. We always had a good time together. My girlfriends were in shock. They had invited us to several parties and social events but we never went. I hadn't been out with them in months. To be honest I really didn't miss it. Or did I?

About eleven months into our relationship Phillip suggested I move in with him. I wasn't really feeling that so I said, "I wouldn't feel comfortable moving in with you. What if we decide to break up? Where would I be?" He said, "I understand." The conversation was dropped. The next month, on Valentine's Day, Phillip asked me to marry him. I was so excited about the "idea" of marriage. I said, "Yes" before I really thought it through. I did know Phillip was a good man, a nice man. He was totally different from any man I had ever been attracted to. The sex was ok but I figured we could work on that. The next thing I knew I was moving in and planning a wedding. Things were happening fast. I was the center of attraction and I loved it.

Before I moved in, Phillip would always have food at his house. I'm not talking carry out or delivery. I mean he would have full course, home cooked meals. His family made sure of that. Even one of the older ladies down the street, a very close friend of the family, would bring him plates and started bringing me plates too.

After I moved in it was a different story. Phillip wanted a home cooked meal every day and he wanted me to cook it. Okay, I didn't have a problem with cooking but everyday might not have been the goal to set for me unless he wanted to be disappointed. I had a very demanding job and that just was not going to work out for me. Oh I tried at first but it got old real quick.

You would have never thought something like missing a day or two of cooking would upset a man to the extent it upset Phillip. We argued over it and I said, "If you want me to cook every day, sit me down. I mean make it so I don't have to work and I'll have your dinner on the table every night. Other than that please shut up talking to me about a damn home cooked meal. As a matter of fact call your people and have them cook you something." What did I say that for? We argued all night and the next day, which was a Saturday.

I needed a break. I called my girlfriends and asked what the plans were for the night. It was the strangest thing. It was as if I was out of the girlfriend club. They were very slow in telling me what they were doing that evening. They were saying things like "Are you sure you want to go out?" "Maybe you need to stay home and work things out." "Phillip is a good man." They were pissing me off. Just when I needed them they were backing away or that's how I felt. I finally got the information from my girlfriend, diarrhea mouth Diane, that's what we called her behind her back because she couldn't hold water. They were meeting at one of our old favorites. It was a small club but had the best mixed drinks and music. I told Phillip I was going out with my girlfriends. He said he didn't mind. Before I left he kissed me and told me how nice I looked.

Man we had a great time. We laughed, talked, danced, drank, and just had a good ole time. We left the club and went to a 24-hour restaurant and had breakfast. I got home about 2:00 a.m.

I went to the bathroom, took the make-up off my face and showered. I got in the bed and tried to snuggle up to Phillip. He moved all the way toward the wall away from me. I sat up in the bed and said, "What's wrong?" He said, "Did you have a good time?" I said, "Yeah. Why are you moving away from me like you don't want me to touch you?" He said, "Nothing", turned over and went to sleep. At this point I was tired of arguing and said, "Okay, good night."

The next day Phillip was fine. We were back to ourselves. A few weeks later my friend, Cynthia, had a birthday party. I asked Phillip to make sure he didn't plan anything because we were going to Cynthia's birthday party. He said, "Cool." He laid out what he was going to wear the day before and went to the barbershop for a haircut and mustache trim. We arrived at the party and if I do say so myself, we were looking mighty fine.

I have always been very sociable so I was all around the party talking to people I hadn't seen in months. I introduced Phillip to a lot of the people. Some the guys were attempting to strike up a conversation with Phillip but he just gave short answers. It was obvious he wasn't interested in what they were saying and seemed a bit uncomfortable. When Cynthia came over to where we were standing to say hello, Phillip gave her a half smile, leaned over and whispered in my ear, "I'm going to find seats."

Phillip led me back to one of the three tables in the whole place that only accommodated two people. I asked him if he wanted to sit with some of my friends at one of the larger tables. He said he would rather sit at the table he chose. Whatever. I was out with my man. We were looking good and I was rather proud. My friends were there, the music was bumping and the food looked delicious. I was frantic. I felt like I had been locked away and this was my first day of release. I just kept bouncing to the music and said, "Okay, this is fine."

About an hour into the party Phillip asked if I was ready to go. I said, "No, the party hasn't even started yet." He said, "Okay, we'll stay." I went to the bar to get a drink and I noticed Phillip was just sitting at the table for two looking like a dejected introvert. I ordered a Grey Goose, cranberry juice and piece of lime for myself and a beer for Phillip and went back to the table. I had taken two sips of my drink and Phillip asked, "Are you ready to go yet?" I just thought forget it and said, "Okay, let's go." I was not going to listen to that all night. Anyway, he wasn't the going out type. I knew that. He made an effort. I could respect that. We gave Cynthia her gift and said our goodbyes. I didn't even get a chance to eat any of Cynthia's mom's famous Lasagna or seafood salad. They really were to die for.

Over the next month, I struggled with the reality that although Phillip was a good man he wasn't the man for me. I had to ask the tough question. Could I live the rest of my life like this? Just one of the questions I should have contemplated before I got all caught up in the euphoria of being married. Two months after the birthday party I told Phillip I had some real concerns about our relationship. We talked for hours.

We agreed we loved each other but forever was not in the stars for us. We just weren't a good match. Our differences would eventually divide us. They were at the crux of who we were as individuals. I love being around people. I love talking to people. I'm not the domesticated type. Phillip, on the other hand, could care less about parties, talking to strangers, going out, etc. He has his circle of family and friends he keeps close. His expectations were more than I could live up too. There was no right or wrong. We had a cordial parting of the ways. Today Phillip is married with four children and has a wonderful life. We are still friends.

Insight

Sometimes you get really tired of dating. In this particular case, I had gotten so tired that I was willing to deny who I really was and look beyond whom Phillip was to live some made up fairy tale in my head. I look back now and think I had to be out of my mind. How long did I actually think it would last? Had things gotten so desperate that I was willing to live a lie? This had to be the most boring relationship I had ever had. At first it was a great respite. It was easy and comfortable. I let it go much too far. I needed a break not a marriage. Not much about the relationship was who I really was. I was settling.

How ridiculous was it for me to pretend Phillip's lifestyle was mine. Sometimes, true opposites do attract. Phillip was a homebody. Phillip was attractive to many women. He was kind, considerate and family-oriented. I could not change him into who I wanted him to be and shouldn't have wanted to. I had accepted his proposal of marriage, which meant I should have been accepting him the way he was forever.

Introducing Phillip to outgoing people and hoping some of their social skills rubbed off on him wasn't going to work. He wasn't going to become more social by osmosis. I wasted a lot of Phillip's and my time living in a fantasy. I think I'll always feel guilty about that.

I had to look at who we were. I liked going out, socializing, and doing things in groups. I couldn't imagine being truly happy without being surrounded by people. I love people. Phillip liked doing things as a couple and occasionally attending family functions. Aretha Franklin said Phillip's way was the only way to go. She proclaimed a long time ago she didn't want "nobody" always sitting around her and her man. Neither did I but I didn't want to feel like a hermit, cut off from the world. You see, it shouldn't have been an inconvenience for me to spend the majority of my time with my man, my future husband. I shouldn't have mind his way because it should have been our way. But, I was who I was and he was who he was. I'm just glad I had enough sense to fess up before I said, 'I do."

ANGELA

Myles - The So Many Signs Man

Myles was a successful businessman, very sure about himself and his choices in life or so he said. He was always very neat and well scrubbed. He is very dark with perfectly white teeth. He graduated from high school but didn't feel the need to go to college. He had money and believed the way to keep it was to keep making it work for him by keeping it moving. He was always so afraid of losing his money and being poor. He would always quote a line from the movie South Central "A fool can't make no money in school." I thought this was so ignorant. I went to college. I believed in education. I know school's not for everyone but that comment always bothered me.

I met Myles in a casino. I was sitting there minding my business and pushing the button hoping for that big win. As I took a sip off of my Bud Light the man next to me said, "You're playing too high. You're never gonna hit." I looked at him and said, "I see you're playing low and I haven't heard your machine ringing yet." He laughed and said "Show you right." He introduced himself and said, "I'm visiting and just came out to have some fun but this shit is pissing me the fuck off." I replied, "Show you right." We both laughed and he offered to buy me another Bud as I took my last sip.

Myles decided to leave to go play the tables. We said our goodbyes. A short time later, Myles came back and said, "It was nice talking to you. I hope the one armed bandit is good to you. He leaned over and slid a hundred dollar bill in my machine and left another Bud. Now I was trying to act like strange men slid hundred dollar bills in my machine all the time and this wasn't no thang. I said, "Thank you. It was nice meeting you and I hope you have a nice visit." He replied, "I can come back and he gave me his phone number and walked away."

I couldn't wait for him to leave. I didn't want him to see what I was really feeling. As soon as he was out of sight, I did a little victory dance in my seat, cashed out at ninety dollars and called it a night. I only had thirty dollars and a few singles for a couple of beers when I got to the casino. I was excited all the way home. All kind of thoughts were racing through my mind - should I call or shouldn't I call. He's not even from here. All the better for me. I would only have to be bothered once in a while. Recently divorced, you better believe I was enjoying single life to the fullest. I started thinking if I call, when should I call. I didn't want to seem frantic or like a gold digger. Then I thought was he trying to bait me? Was he playing a game? Well, I guess I needed to dust off the old game playing skills and get to work. I used to be the master. I decided to call him in two to three days and allow the phone to ring for no more than three times. He answered on the second ring. Maybe he was serious.

Myles and I started talking long distance. He was six hours away from me. We had great conversations and surprisingly had a lot in common. By the third week Myles was on his way back to visit me. We met at another casino. We had lunch, gambled for a while and went back to his room and talked for a couple of hours. Before I left he asked if he could kiss me good-bye and I was more than willing to oblige. It was a very nice and gentle kiss. Two months into the relationship he asked if I would meet him at a casino almost two hours from me. I said, "Sure." I got my hair, nails, and eyebrows done. I went shopping and bought the cutest little outfits and was on my way.

When I arrived he had perfume wrapped in pretty packaging waiting for me. He opened up a suitcase with ten thousand dollars in it and said, "O.k. baby, let's go have some fun." I thought wait a damn minute. Sirens and red flashing lights started going off in my head. I sat on the bed stunned and looking very serious. I said, "Myles where did you get that money? What do you really do? Now you said you have investments. What kind of investments and is it illegal? I'm not going anywhere with you until you prove to me you're not a drug dealer, thief or some other criminal." He couldn't stop laughing. He called his brothers and one of his sisters to tell them about my reaction. His younger brother found it to be hilarious. His other brothers and sister were rather perturbed he would call with such silliness but each confirmed he was not a criminal and explained where and how they came by their wealth. I felt a whole lot better. I drank some of the Korbel and was ready to roll. We had so much fun that night. I still didn't sleep with him even though he tried all the right moves to get me to. Believe me it wasn't easy saying no – all that money, drinks, and those pearly whites. Yeah I had to really focus and keep saying in my mind – I'm not a ho, I'm not a ho, I'm not a ho.

I later found out Myles was very judgmental. When it came to women sleeping around and sexing too soon, he immediately categorized them as sluts. He even told me he was testing me that night and if I had slept with him he would have lost all respect for me. Yeah, right. We began to take our relationship serious. We were moving a little quick for my taste but he was a man of conviction. He seemed so sure about what he wanted and that was me. I decided why not give it a try. If nothing else it would be an interesting ride. We decided we would be exclusive even with the long distance. Some weeks later, Myles sent for me to visit him at his home. I didn't know exactly what to wear. I had so much shit it wasn't funny. I had to borrow a suitcase from my best friend. I took a week off of work, packed my bags and boarded a flight. Everything was great, wonderful even but I still couldn't figure out why he didn't have a woman. He was nice looking, could hold a conversation about more than sports or the latest news about some celebrity, and had a nice personality. It wasn't long. I soon found out.

I made it to my destination. Myles greeted me with flowers and a whole itinerary for the week. We arrived at his place. It was a little smaller than I had expected but decorated beautifully. I wasn't in his home for ten minutes before he started laying out the house rules.

Sign number one. Oh my God. How didn't I pick up Myles was an anal retentive neat freak? Don't hang the towels here when you get out of the shower put them here, don't leave the sink dirty, wash your plate after you finish, we'll make the bed every morning as soon as we're up, and on and on and on. I was like damn. I myself had been known to go overboard about putting things in their place but this shit was ridiculous. Well, I was there so I had to deal with it. The first two days were fun. We just hung out. Myles showed me the downtown area and all around the city. The third day crazy reared its ugly head.

Sign number two. We went to Dave and Buster's. I had never been there and although he had plans to go to a restaurant downtown I really didn't feel like getting dressed up. He agreed. When we got there we ordered something to eat and decided to play the games. I was watching him play a game. He was winning and seemed to be having a good time. I was standing beside him cheering him on. Oh, he was eating it up. I decided I would buy a few tokens and find a game to play. I said, "I'll be right back". I found a game and started playing. I was having a great time when Myles came around the corner looking meaner than a junkyard dog. He said in a deep, mean, even tone, "Where have you been? I've been looking all over for you?" The place wasn't even that big. The way he looked at me made me uneasy. You could tell if he thought he could get away with it he would have knocked the hell out of me right then and there. I calmly looked at him, smiled and said, "What are you talking about? I'm right here, right behind you, in the next row playing a game." He started to walk away and said, "Come on, let's go." I was thinking is he for real? This was some stupid shit. Did he actually want me to stay right by his side and watch him play? That shit ain't no fun. By the time we reached the truck, he had calmed down and everything seemed to be good again.

The next day Myles had to check on a couple of his businesses. We got up early, he finished what he had to do and we were on our way. We had scheduled massages at a spa not

far from his home. Sign number three. We
stopped at a cell phone shop and went in. Myles
started talking to the sales representative. The
representative tried to include both of us in the
conversation so he directed his answers at both
of us. Myles seemed really uneasy and started
to fidget with something on the counter. All of a
sudden in the middle of the salesman's sentence
Myles said, "I changed my mind. Let's go." I
asked him what was wrong. He replied, "That
motherfucker was all in your face. I'm the one
buying the damn phone but he wants to be all in
your face and disrespect me." I said, "Huh." He
said, "And oh you were enjoying it, can't take
you nowhere." I just knew he was kidding but
this incident came up in several subsequent
conversations. For all that confidence Myles
tried to make sure you knew he had, he was
really insecure and had some serious trust
issues. We made it to the spa and Lord knows I
needed it. Myles was turning out to be a whole
lotta work and hell I already had a nine to five.

Later that day we were relaxing and
enjoying a glass of wine. We were way smoothed
out. We were cuddling and hugging and I knew
tonight was going to be the night that we gave
ourselves to each other. And it was. It was
nothing to talk about. It was far from horrible
but wasn't tipping the Richter scale either.

On the fifth day I got up really early. I was
leaving the next day. I tried to wake Myles but
he was dead to the world. I decided I would

walk down to the convenience store about two
blocks away. It was a beautiful day. There was
a gentle warm breeze and the sun was shining.
Sign number four. I walked back in the house
and all hell broke loose. Myles began ranting
and raving about me leaving the house and not
letting him know I was leaving. Actually it was a
little more than ranting and raving he was
talking very loud and pacing back and forth
through the house like a lunatic. Now this was
it. I cussed that motherfucker out for everything
he was worth and then some. He just looked at
me like I had lost my mind and said, "I'm sorry I
was just worried. I didn't know what happened.
You scared me. You're leaving tomorrow and I'm
beginning to feel all fucked up inside. Damn, I
done messed around and fell in love with you."

That little sorry didn't calm me down
though. I was pissed. And the falling in love
didn't faze me either. I had been in and out of
love lots of times. He spent the whole day trying
to make up. We decided to take a ride. We
drove about an hour. On the way back to his
house we stopped at a roadside rest area. Myles
went to the restroom and I sat on one of the
benches and waited for him. I think being
outside finally calmed me down. As soon as I
calmed down Myles said something to piss me
off again. He wanted me to say I loved him too.
I wasn't in love with him so I didn't think it was
fair to say it if it wasn't true. Now he was pissed
and said, "Let's go." I didn't say anything. I

followed him to the car and got in. He started playing Al Green. Neither of us said a word. Myles finally broke the silence by saying, "Why would you get involved with me if you can't love me?" Okay, crazy as hell. I said, "Wait we've been dating for a little more than four months. Why are you rushing things?" He said, "What time is your flight? We need to make sure you're on it." I said, "Pull the car over. I think I'm going to be sick." He pulled over, I got out of the car and told him to take his crazy ass on and I'd get a way to get my things. I started walking toward a gas station. Myles was driving slowly beside me pleading with me to get back in the car. I finally got back in. Myles was laughing his ass off and said, "Damn, I like you girl." All I could think was too much work and too much drama. All I could do that evening was sleep. I was so ready to leave.

The day I was leaving, Myles got up early, cooked breakfast, woke me up and presented me with the most beautiful bouquet of roses. Everything was going fine. I got up from the table and helped clean the kitchen. I went into the bedroom to pack my things. Myles came in the bedroom and said, "Why don't you leave some of your things here. You'll be back right?" I said, "I'll be back but I'm going to take my things." Myles got real quiet and said, "Would you mind if I didn't go to the airport?" I said, "No problem." Oh my God, why did I say that?

Sign number five. That fool started pacing back and forth saying, "I knew you didn't love me. You just want me for the things I can do for you. And whose suitcase is that? It doesn't match your others. Some old broke ass man probably gave it to you." I said, "What is wrong with you? That's my girlfriends' suitcase. Before I could say anything else he said, "Fuck that bitch." Okay crossing the line. I went the hell off aaaaannndddd complete silence again.

The limo pulled up and I was never so ready to get away from a situation than I was that day. When I arrived at the airport Myles was standing at the entrance. I had about two hours before my flight left so we went into Chili's and talked. I guess this was confession time for him. He professed his love, apologized, talked about how scared he was in the relationship, and asked that I please give him another chance. I didn't give him an answer at that moment. I told him I would call him when I got back home. Now I needed some advice. I called my mother and conference called my best friend and three other girlfriends. My mother said, "Get away from him, he sounds like he has a real problem." My best friend and girlfriends couldn't see past the money and said I should give him another chance. They all agreed I had a very low "shit happens in relationships" tolerance level.

I returned Myles calls a couple of days later. He called at least ten times a day since I had left. We talked. I told him I was willing to give the relationship another chance if he agreed to think about what he says to me before he opens his mouth and tried trusting me. About two weeks later, Myles started trying to persuade me to quit my job. He wanted me to move in with him. He offered to pay me whatever I was making on my job. I kept trying to explain to him I didn't go to college to sit at home. I wanted to contribute something to the world. He just couldn't understand. He would often say, "Do you know what some women would give to have a man offer what I'm offering you?"

Sign number six. I met Myles a month later at the casino two hours away again. We were really happy to see each other. We ate, had a couple of drinks in the players club and went to the casino. He gave me money to play with and said he'd be back after he played the tables for a while. When he came back, I was sitting at a machine talking to a very young guy who was telling me his tragic life story. Myles came over and said to the young man, "That's my woman you're talking to. I think you better move your ass on." I was so embarrassed. The young man had just gotten out of the hospital and had been diagnosed with HIV. He still had the hospital identification bracelet on. He just wanted someone to talk to and this ignorant fool acted so ugly towards him. I apologized to the young man for Myles rudeness, cashed out my ticket, and started heading toward the hotel room.

Myles was behind me asking what was wrong. I couldn't even talk. We got on the elevator and he said with a very devilish grin, "Girl, you gonna make me knock the hell out of you." I had always been a fighter. I grew up fighting. I didn't want to fight Myles. I believed if you have to get physical with the person you're in a relationship with then you don't need to be in the relationship. But, I was not going to let him bully me. I replied, "Try it and I'll be mailing your dick to your family in pieces." He laughed so hard, he was crying. I thought what the hell?

Sign number seven. We slept together that night but the sex was quite different than before. Every move was to demonstrate control. It was if he was letting me know he was in control and all I needed to do was submit. Sometimes I like a man to take charge but this was more than that. At first I thought maybe he was trying to improve on his previous mediocre performance but no that wasn't it. The next day I left and decided our relationship was not going to work out. I had to figure a way out. It was apparent leaving Myles was not going to be an easy task.

Over the next few weeks, I gradually stopped calling or returning Myles' calls. The last day before I finally let Myles know our relationship was over, he called me back to back to back and so on and so on. I was in a four-hour meeting at work. He was calling so much. I started thinking something was seriously wrong. I called him and he said, "Hi, I miss you." Oh Lord now what. I replied, "Hi, what's wrong?" He said, "Nothing. What took you so long to call me back?" I replied, "I was in a meeting." Sign number eight. He replied, "Fuck them motherfuckers, when I call you need to call me back. It don't make no damn sense to be in a meeting for four hours and I bet ya'll didn't get shit accomplished." Now he was stepping all over my toes, disrespecting my profession and commenting on shit he had no idea about. We had a heated argument and I hung up the phone in his face but not before telling him how ignorant and insecure he was. The next morning I told him I didn't want to be in a relationship with him and a few other choice words. I had had an encounter with the OOOWEE man the night before. It was over for me. The next week Myles showed up at my door with flowers and that perfect smile. I was not moved. Myles still calls every three to six months to ask, "Why did we break up again? And "Do you still love me?" What? CRAZY!

Insight
I believe a woman should support her man and a man his woman but I didn't have the time or energy for Myles. Myles was a real trip and the ride was something like I had never experienced. Don't get me wrong. I like a confident man but there is a significant difference between a confident man and a

controlling man who is always afraid he's not going to be in control so he tries to bully his woman into submission. I wasn't willing or able to submit to Myles in the way he wanted. It was clear Myles wanted me to spend all of my time soothing his insecurities and making him the center of my life. He wanted me to please him as if he was the reason I was born into this world. Some may be willing and able to do anything for money but a man like Myles would never be fully content unless he is in total control of your every move. He will even want to control your thoughts.

Money isn't enough in a relationship. I worked. I could provide for myself. Of course, I didn't have the kind of money Myles had but I wasn't starving either. The things we could buy, places we could go, and the peace of mind that came with being financially stable was undeniably a plus but all these things weren't worth my sanity. I thought what Myles was asking, what he expected was in one word – crazy. I should have listened to my mother and got as far away from Myles as I could when I first saw the signs of crazy.

ANGELA

Dylan - The OOOWEE Man

Dylan is a hardworking man with a rock hard body and smooth, flawless skin. The man can make your toes curl and send chills up and down your spine when you just think about him. Just his touch and a deep stare into your eyes can transport your mind and spirit to a place where all is good in the world. He has chiseled features and a smile that can make the devil submit and close hell down. He is very independent and asks you for nothing but your time and enjoys his freedom as a single man. Dylan does not believe in the institution of marriage even though he comes from a very religious family who frowns on his lifestyle. He believes in commitment but does not have the desire to marry.

I met Dylan at a concert. He was sitting three seats over from me. I saw him during intermission staring at me but I was with my girls so I didn't pay him much attention. At the end of the concert I heard a sweet low deep voice say, "Excuse me. What's your name?" I turned around and it was Dylan. I smiled and said, "Why?" He immediately replied, "It's my birthday and you and your girls look like you're having a lot of fun. I'm here by myself and wondered where you all were going after the concert. I'm not ready to go home." I told him my name and that we were going to a new club. I gave him the name of the club and said, "Happy birthday. I hope you have a good one".

When we made it to the club we found a table, ordered drinks and partied like we were going to turn ourselves in at the county jail the next morning. A manager for one of the groups performing at the concert sent drinks over to our table and eventually came over and introduced himself. He asked me to dance. After the dance he asked if I would sit and talk with him at his table. I did.

After our brief conversation, I had to get back with my girls. I told him I'd talk to him later. He said, "just in case here's my phone number. Call me if you're interested in getting to know me better because I sure want to get to know you". A short while later Dylan walked in with the prettiest powder blue hat on. Man he was wearing that hat. He didn't come over to the table but he sent drinks. He walked to the other side of the club where they were shooting pool.

As the night went on we drank, partied and danced. We knew we were going to feel it but tonight was one of those nights where everything was right and the consequences felt the next day were going to be well worth it.

Around 2:00 a.m. my girl's phones started ringing - the booty calls were in effect. They started peeling off one by one. They all left except one girlfriend visiting from out of town.

She was talking with some guy she had been dancing with for the last three or four songs. I decided to go over and talk with the manager. Actually, I had forgotten all about Dylan until he walked up and stood right in the middle of the manager and me and asked me, "Who is this? He with the band?" I was shocked and replied, "I don't know you. You better get the hell out of my business." He just smiled and said, "Can I walk you to your car when you're ready to go"? I ignored him and continued my conversation with the manager who found the whole situation to be hilarious and couldn't stop laughing and mocking Dylan saying "He with the band?"

Well the night was almost over. The manager and I said our goodbyes and I promised I would call him the next week. He lived in Colorado and traveled a lot. I told him I would leave a message with my information. Out of the corner of my eye I could see Dylan sitting at a side table drinking a beer. When the manager left, Dylan walked over and asked if he could walk me to my car again but this time he brought the owners of the club with him to vouch for his character. I agreed. We talked a little while. Before we said goodbye, he gave me his home and cell numbers and email address.

When I met Dylan I was in a relationship with Myles. The guy you just read about. I really wasn't looking for a relationship although I knew my relationship with Myles was on very shaky ground. Oh hell, truth be told I knew it wasn't going to last. The control issue was way too much for me. After that relationship, I didn't want to be in any relationship.

Six months later, Myles and I had just had a huge argument. I had called Dylan a few times since we had met. We had gone out for drinks and dinner and even went to the beach where we talked for hours. There was absolutely no physical contact except for a very sweet kiss on the cheek. The night of my big argument with Myles, I decided to call Dylan and ask if he wanted to meet for drinks and dinner at the Mexican restaurant we met at the last time we went out. He was excited and said he was just thinking about me and we should meet around 8:00 p.m. because he had some things he had to do for his sister.

We arrived at the restaurant at the same time. He smiled and all the frustration I had seemed to melt away. We ate and talked for about two hours. He suddenly cut me off in the middle of my sentence and said, "I've wanted you since the first day I saw you." I replied, "Okay, let's go." He got nervous and knocked the napkins and silverware on the floor as he was calling for the waiter to bring the check. We left and went to a hotel. I wasn't expecting much.   I wasn't expecting anything.   I just needed to be held and caressed if only for one night.

Held. Caressed. Yeah! I got that and so much more. The man opened me up like I didn't know. Now I had my share of men but this was different. He was gentle and loving and so full of passion.   Words wouldn't do justice to what went on in that room.   All I could say was OOOWEE. The next morning Myles called. He started in on me immediately.   He wanted to know where I had been, whom I was with, what was wrong with me, had I lost my mind, and so on and so on.   I was standing in an Old Navy clothing store. I was speechless for a moment. I told him to hold on.   I went outside and screamed to the top of my lungs, "It's over. Don't call me anymore." I felt like the character Richie Vento in the movie 'Harlem Nights' after he had sex with Sunshine.

Dylan and I began dating and were practically inseparable after that night. Myles tried all he knew to get back together. I wasn't having it. The last time I saw Myles was at a casino. He had called and asked that I meet him to talk. He said he needed closure. My friends did not want me to go. They didn't trust him and thought he might hit me, slap me or physically hurt me in some other way. I went anyway. When I think about that now, it really wasn't a smart thing to do. Myles had never hit me but he had all the traits of a crazed, jealous,

killer boyfriend.   When we met Myles was a
complete gentleman. We spent the night in the
same room. Separate beds. We talked most of
the night. We parted on good terms. He asked
for a last kiss. We kissed. I could feel his hurt
but I couldn't let myself get drawn in. I layed
across the bed and fell asleep. Myles went to the
casino to gamble.

      The next morning we ate breakfast and I
left. When I got back to town I went straight
over to Dylan's house. I was so anxious to see
him. When I got there he was sitting in the den
watching television. I went to hug him and he
was kind of cold. I asked, "What's wrong?" He
replied, "I thought you were going to talk. Why
did you have to spend the night?" He was truly
hurt. I could see the hurt in his eyes. We talked
for hours. I explained it was over between me
and Myles and nothing sexual happened
between us. It wasn't until I placed my hand on
the bible and swore this to be true that Dylan
got all right. We had hot, passionate, I'm still
kind of mad but I love you sex on the floor of the
den. I never told him I kissed Myles and prayed
for a long time I would be forgiven for placing my
hand on that Bible.

      Dylan and I moved in together a year later.
We had fun together. We loved each other.
Dylan didn't ask for much. He believed in
commitment and expected me to be committed
to him. That's what that first night of intimacy
and every minute after that was all about. It

was if Dylan came into my life just when I needed him. He was a much-needed breath of fresh air after Myles. He was a welcomed distraction from the craziness I had just experienced in my previous relationship. Dylan helped me see clearer what I truly wanted in my man and my relationship.

Our relationship was good for a while. As time went on I started thinking about marriage. I knew Dylan's views on marriage but I felt if he loved me enough he would marry me. Even though I knew Dylan was a free spirit who rebelled against all things traditional or conventional and was not going to be tamed or contained, I believed in our love more and knew if Dylan loved me enough he would change his views on marriage. I wanted more. I wanted security. I wanted to be married. I wanted Dylan to marry me.

I received all kinds of advice. From you know he loves you be satisfied with that to leave Dylan and the relationship. I wasn't going to give up on Dylan. I guess I could have said happy is happy and damn all the rest. Except for the issue of marriage, I was happy. I didn't want to judge his love for me by whether or not he would marry me. Somewhere deep down in my soul I knew he genuinely cared for me. However, the struggle between our beliefs and desires would eventually create an emotional conflict in me that was too big for my love for him to endure.

Questions of wasn't I good enough to marry, did his heart truly belong to someone else, if he met someone else would he marry her, was I just safe, and why was he truly resistant to marriage were constantly on my mind. He had never given me a real answer to the last question except that of being rebellious towards the wishes of his family.

Dylan took a job that kept him away from home three to four consecutive days a week. It was during these times my mind wandered the most. It was the worst feeling.

One of those days I was sitting on our patio racking my brain with questions and reasons why Dylan would jeopardize our relationship for the sake of rebelling against his family's wishes and his mirage-like image of institutionalized commitment. I started to feel my heart racing, I felt hot, and I could feel my pulse in my throat. This couldn't be good. I had never had an anxiety attack but I was sure this was it. I had to calm down. That day I realized I had to take an examination of myself. I needed to stop focusing on why he didn't want to get married. Dylan was very clear on what he wanted. He was satisfied. I needed to focus on why I was being so careless with my own happiness; why was I placing all bets on Dylan possibly changing his mind; what is it that I wanted; and what would make me happy. I did that.

Over the course of a year, after many tears and a power struggle between my mind and my heart, I made the decision to leave Dylan. It was more difficult than I had ever imagined. My heart so desperately wanted me to stay. I loved him. In the end, I decided my heart needed something and someone else. During that year, things went on as usual but I was so sad inside.

When I told Dylan I was leaving he couldn't understand my reasoning. He laughed and told me I needed to stop being so dramatic. With that one statement my feelings, concerns, and insecurities were flicked away like a piece of lint from his shoulder. I thought was he blind, couldn't he see my sadness? I left and moved into a small apartment on the other side of town. Dylan tried for over a year to get me to come back. I told him the only way I would come back was as his wife. He stopped trying after he came by my apartment and unexpectedly saw my date and I walking to the car holding hands.

Today I am married to a wonderful man. The same man Dylan saw at my apartment complex. He is the culmination of Myles without the crazy and Dylan. He is compassionate, loving, understanding, confidant, and financially stable. We have been married for seven years. Dylan's sister told me he never married. He has lived with the same woman for over five years. Ain't that something? I guess he never changed his views on marriage. I wonder if he ever thinks of me, our relationship, and/or the way it ended. Dylan could only give me a part of what I needed. I still think about Dylan every now and then but the memories fade more and more with each passing year. My husband makes sure of that.

Insight

I loved Dylan. I know Dylan loved me. No matter how much we might want it to be, sometimes love just isn't enough. Compromising is a part of any relationship but when it comes to compromising yourself and who you are that's a different story. I also had to realize I just wasn't as strong as I had always prided myself in being. I thought I could handle anything. My favorite saying was "it's not that serious, just deal with it". Unfortunately, strength has little to do with fending off love and the emotions that come along with it.

In the beginning, that surreal feeling love offers when you're consciously aware you're falling in love is undeniable. It's insatiable. It's the feeling you get when you're falling in love for the first time as a teenager. Something you thought you would never feel again. When he's around you feel safe, warm, and even a bit giddy. You think about your love when he's not around, you wonder what he's doing and where he is, you wonder if he's thinking about you as much as you're thinking about him and then the phone rings and it's him. Confirmations that your love is true are all around you like an unexpected hug or kiss, a gentle touch, or small tokens expressing his love for you.

As time goes on you try desperately to hold on to those feelings but when all of your needs aren't being met time happens. Memories are eroded and the grip you used to hold on so tightly to those memories with weakens. Although I tried not to allow them in, insecurities began to flood my mind when Dylan was there and when he wasn't. Unanswered questions swam around in my head constantly. They kept slapping me in my face. I couldn't deny them. They were a part of me. I believed in marriage. I believed when two people fall in love they should be married. We were already living together why not make it official. The love I had for Dylan couldn't outweigh my beliefs.

Growing up I heard people say, "Time will tell.", "Give it time.", and "In time." I had never applied these sayings to love or relationships until Dylan. Time allowed me to see Dylan. Time allowed me to see me. Time allowed me to see us. I gave us time and in time the story was told. It didn't matter why Dylan did not want to get married. What mattered was why I was trying to force him into a marriage with me. He was clear from the beginning. It's interesting how you go from loving a person unconditionally to just change this or that to prove your love for me.

Leaving Dylan was the most difficult decision I had ever made in my life. We had been together for five years. I realized I was living Dylan's life and not mine. After three years into the relationship, when I knew I was having a problem with Dylan's position on marriage and that he was not going to change his views, I should have been strong. I should have been strong enough to leave. But, I wasn't. I didn't want to. I wanted to fix it when there was nothing to be fixed. He had his beliefs and I had mine. That should have been enough. That should have been okay.

William - The Married Man

William is 6'2, very handsome, and built like an Olympic hurdler. Although he does not have an ounce of fat on his body he never exercises. William has been educated at the best schools and universities in the country. He grew up poor and his family was determined he would have the best education money could buy no matter the cost. They worked hard to make sure he had everything he needed to be successful.

William grew up with his grandfather, aunt and brother. His mother died of cancer when he was very young. She was a quiet woman and was very involved in the church. Her father was the minister of the church in the small town they lived in. William said he couldn't remember much about his mother only that there were what seemed like hundreds of people at her funeral. William's father was from the same small town. William's grandfather did not approve of his mother and father's relationship so his mother ran off with his father and married him when she was eighteen. When

she became pregnant she returned home with
no idea of where her husband was.

When William's older brother was two
years old his mother and father reunited. They
moved to a small town about thirty miles away
from where they grew up. After William's mother
became pregnant with him, William's father
disappeared again leaving her alone, pregnant
with a small child and little to nothing to eat.
William's mother called her father.   His
grandfather told his mother the only way she
could return home was to promise she would not
have anything to do with her husband. She
agreed. His father would come by every now and
then with toys and gifts for William and his
brother and whatever little bit of money he had
for William's mother. They never divorced but
never lived together again.

William's father was never a constant in
his life. Until William was eleven years old he
believed his father left home in search of a better
job in another state. Years later he found out his
father died a year after his mother died. The
truth was William's father left the state because
he was on the run from the police after being
involved in a robbery that left a man paralyzed.
William believed his minister grandfather and
aunt did not tell him and his brother the truth
until they were older because the whole ordeal
was an embarrassment to the family. Although
his grandfather and aunt never made any
negative remarks about his father to him or his

brother, they always felt their grandfather and aunt never liked their father and maybe even loathed him. William and his brother would often talk about it.

When William's brother was sixteen he was involved in a fatal car accident. He and some friends had been drinking and decided to drag race in an open field. Kids always drag raced there but this particular time his brother's old beater hit a large rock and flipped over. He was the only one in the car.

After his brother's death William said he became very quiet, introverted. When people would comment on how quiet he was his grandfather would always remark, "He's just like his mother." William said that really wasn't it. He just felt so alone after his brother's death. His only confidant had been taken away. Although it may never have been said directly to him, William felt the teachings of the church made him feel like his mother, father and brother had all been punished because they had not lived the way God intended. He said he always felt fearful inside.

William tried to be a good boy. He always did what was asked of him. He never talked back. He got excellent grades in school. He had a couple of girlfriends during high school but did not fornicate. He became known as the good little church boy. He said he focused on doing what was right so he wouldn't be punished.

When he graduated from high school he received twelve letters of acceptance to colleges and universities from across the country. He became the example for all young kids in his small community. Everyone was so proud of him. He was even in the town's newspaper. William decided to go to a University 1200 miles away that offered him a partial scholarship for all four years because it had exactly what he wanted to major in and was well known for it. His grandfather and aunt weren't too pleased with his decision but supported him anyway.

When he arrived at school he met his roommate and took a tour of the campus. He said he was shocked, amazed, and for the first time in a long time really happy. During his first four years of college, William made lots of new friends; joined a fraternity; reinvented himself; and became a party animal. Before this William had not even as much as taken a sip of beer. Now he was drinking, smoking marijuana, and having sex regularly. He was no longer the good little church boy. William never wanted to leave so he always made sure he kept up with his schoolwork. William went on to get a Bachelor of Science, Master of Business Administration, and a Doctor of Philosophy in Communications.

After he attained his master's degree, he married a girl he met in college. They moved back to his grandfather's home for a short time. His new wife complained constantly and wanted to leave what she termed "the God-forsaken place." Things weren't the same for William either. It was if he was too big for the small town. He said he felt like he was suffocating. He was anxious and began to feel alone and sad again. He said he began to hate it because there was just too much pain there. William began to apply for jobs back in the state he had attended college. Times were very hard. He wasn't getting any callbacks. He then decided to enter into the Ph.D. program at his old University. Of course he was accepted.

William's grandfather was very disappointed in his decision to go so far away from home again. William's aunt tried to talk him out of his decision. Three months later William and his new wife were on their way, 1200 miles away. William and his wife lived in married student housing for the first two years while he worked on his Ph.D. Somewhere during the third year of marriage William's wife left him for another man. William was crushed. A month later William's aunt called from her retirement home to tell him his grandfather was ill and didn't have much time to live. These events sent William into a tailspin. He dropped out of the Ph.D. program and returned to his grandfather's house. His grandfather died six days after he got there. His wife heard about his grandfather and came to William. William was happy to see her and vowed to forgive her indiscretion. His wife looked him squarely in the eye and said "Sweetie I'm just here for what's mine."

William didn't want to do anything. He started hanging out with some of the town's winos and potheads. He soon graduated to harder drugs. His grandfather had left everything to him. He sold everything in the house to support his habit. He soon sold the house and the few acres the house sat on. He sent part of the money to his soon to be ex-wife. He said the company he sold the house and land to tore the church down. He admitted tearing down the church made him deeply happy.

Soon after, his aunt became ill and asked him to come see her in the hospital. With her last conscious breath, she begged and pleaded with him to get help. As she lay dying, William said it was if all the anger and hurt he had suppressed came roaring up in him like a great flood. Tears began to flow everywhere. He was inconsolable. He was screaming, "No, no, I'll be good". The nurses rushed into the room and soon a doctor gave him a shot to settle him. It took two nurses and three orderlies to hold him down. After his aunt's funeral service, William checked himself into a drug rehabilitation center.

The next semester William was back at the University working on his Ph.D. By the time he completed it his divorce was final. He landed a tenure-track position as a professor at a well-known college teaching Communications in the

School of Business. He worked diligently toward his tenure. He focused on nothing else. He didn't date or go out at all. His whole life was his work. About four years into his job he began to have serious problems with the Chair of his department. He was the only African American in his department. Although he had excellent relationships with his students and always received above average student evaluations, the Chair was on him to publish articles and secure funding for research.

William said he had done both. He had published seven articles and had both state and foundation funded research projects every year he was there. William felt he was always treated as an outsider and was being targeted by the Chair for termination. He was nervous about his fate and angry there was little he could do about his situation unless he had proof he was meeting the standards set by the University for Tenure and the Chair was deliberately trying to thwart his advancement. Over the next year, there was a constant tug of war between him and his Chair. She would try to discount his work and constantly require he do more. During this time he met a woman. She was a social worker and excellent at listening. They became very close and married a year after he became tenured.

I met William at a conference on a global look at ethical issues and communication in the business world. We hit it off right away. I felt safe with him because he was married and I was not looking for anything even resembling a relationship after my divorce. I was going through the tenure phase for the first time. He had a lot of good insight. We talked for hours about his experience and what to look out for. We exchanged business cards before we left. We talked everyday and sometimes twice a day. He told me about his life, his first wife, his current wife, his brother, mother, father, grandfather and aunt. I told him about my childhood, my children, and ex-husband. There were no expectations so we were free to talk about everything. It was no holds barred.

About four months after our first meeting, we realized we would be attending another conference at the same time. We started planning what we were going to do between and after sessions. He seemed to be determined to find a nice lounge or club so I could meet a nice guy. I told him I had been celibate for two years. He thought I was abnormal. I thought it was rather funny coming from someone who grew up in the church. Anyway it would be great to hang out with William again.

William was presenting at the conference so I went to hear his presentation. He was not a great orator but the information was quite interesting. We decided to go to a supper club not far from the conference hotel. It was gorgeous. It even had an upstairs with a dance floor, bar and disc jockey. The music was o.k. It was a mixture of everything: pop, soul, reggae, country, neo-soul, and rock. We ate and decided to go upstairs. One of the guys from the conference was there alone. We invited him to join us. His name was Steve. He was not in Business or Communications but thought the conference sounded interesting so he decided to attend.

Steve hadn't been sitting with us ten minutes before William asked him if he was married. He gave a very definitive yes. William said, "Oh well, another one bites the dust." That began a conversation which lasted almost an hour about marriage. Steve was defending the institution of marriage and William was making the point that it was unnatural for a man to be with only one woman for the rest of his life. I agreed with Steve and told William he should look into open marriages if he believed the crap he was trying to sell us. We laughed and Steve asked me to dance.

When we got back to the table William grabbed my hand and led me back to the dance floor saying, "Oh no you don't, you can't sit down. You have to dance with both of us". By the end of the night I was worn out. We tried all kinds of drinks. We had a great time. The next day, as we were preparing to leave, we promised to keep in touch. Steve was only an hour away from me. We planned to meet so he could introduce me to his wife, Sheri. I met Sheri about a month later. We instantly connected. I finally had a shopping buddy that didn't mind traveling for a sale.

We all talked to each other on a daily basis. On one of our shopping excursions Sheri made a comment about me watching out for William's true intentions. I thought this was rather bold. I asked her what she meant. She told me William had been making comments to Steve. He told Steve he was attracted to me. I responded by saying, "What's wrong with him thinking I am attractive?" She said, "No. You're not hearing me. I don't know all of the details because he refused to tell me. I do know after the last conversation Steve and William had Steve came to me and told me to tell you to watch out for William because he's up to no good." I hate it when people tell you the cleaned up version of a conversation. I said, "I know he told you something or else you wouldn't be telling me any of this. What exactly did Steve say William said?"

Sheri responded by just waving her hand and saying, "Don't say I didn't warn you. But any married man that says he's priming you for bigger and better things to come and doesn't explain what he means does not have your best interest at heart." What Sheri was telling me still sounded a little sketchy or maybe I didn't really want to hear it. I thought William and I had become true friends. He never made a pass at me or spoke out of turn. He knew exactly how I felt about men who cheated on their wives and knew I would want no part of it.

When I got home that evening I had three urgent messages from William. I put my bags down and called him immediately. William was very upset. He had been escorted from campus in handcuffs by the local police for allegedly having a relationship with one of his female students. I almost passed out when he told me the story. Apparently, one of his students filed a sexual harassment charge against him for making sexual remarks and bartering with her for sex in exchange for a higher grade in his class. The charges were later dismissed after the student recanted her story but did nothing to repair William's reputation at the University.

The next six months were absolutely horrific for William. Class enrollment for his courses dropped, colleagues stopped speaking or associating with him and his relationship with his wife suffered. I remained a true friend to William. Although Steve still spoke to William things between them weren't the same. Steve would often call me after he had spoken to William and express his doubts of William's innocence in the situation with the student.

William started applying for teaching positions elsewhere but it was if he had been blackballed. His wife started spending more and more time with a man from work who she said was gay and just her friend. Most of the time William was home alone because he didn't want to take the chance of running into someone from work and getting the quick glance, nasty stare or awkward avoidance.

The strong and confident William I first met was fading fast. He finally got a job with a small marketing firm. He was feeling much better and was ecstatic when a white professor at the University was brought up on the same charges initiated by the same student. It was later found that the student had a mental illness and had made the same accusations towards a teacher at her community college. The professor called William to talk about the devastation he had been through and even though he didn't really know William, he wanted to apologize for assuming the worst of a fellow colleague. He also told William he still held his position in the College of Arts and Sciences and the school, his department and the University fully supported him. William could not wait to call the Chair of his old department. She was not in so he left a message. After several attempts to contact her he decided to take legal action against the University and was advised to stop all communication except through his attorney.

Meanwhile, by William's accounts, his relationship with his wife was becoming strained at best. He began to talk more and more about their relationship. He would often say, "My wife doesn't understand me." I would usually follow with "maybe you're not being clear". Every time I made that statement he would get so mad and say, "Yeah, you women stick together. It's always the man's fault." There would follow a long conversation about men and women and unrealistic expectations.

William's new job brought him to the area in which I was living several times a year. We would meet, talk and go out sometimes. On one visit I couldn't wait to see William to tell him about a man I had met. I was excited to tell him about my first date with him and how nice it was. When we met for dinner I started telling him about my newfound love interest. William was so negative about everything I told him. He kept making jokes and whenever I told him something about him he would ask how I knew that to be true. I stopped the conversation and asked what his problem was. He told me his wife had moved out and was staying with her gay male friend.

I said, "William I am so sorry to hear that. What are you going to do?" He just looked at me. He asked if I were ready to go. I said, "Sure, let's go. Where are we going?" William wanted to go out to a club to have a drink and dance. I was definitely game for that. I hadn't been out dancing in a while. There was a nightclub in the hotel where he was staying, so we decided to go back to his hotel. We danced and got so drunk. We laughed until our sides hurt. William insisted I stay in his room and get a couple hours of sleep before I drove home. I felt safe with him.

We got back to the room and I went to the
bathroom. When I came out the door William
pulled me close and kissed me. I pushed him
back and asked what he was doing. He was
married or did he forget. I should have left then
but I didn't. I moved past him and sat on the
bed. William came over and stood in front of me
with his crouch in my face. He said, "Come on.
Let's just do it one time. No one will ever know."
I went to get up but William pushed me back
onto the bed. As he lay on top of me, he started
kissing me on my neck and whispered, "Please,
just one time." I could feel his erection through
his pants. He began to kiss my ears, face and
finally my lips. I had been celibate for almost
five years and this was definitely the wrong
position to be in. I couldn't say no. I wanted it
as much as he did. I wanted him. All of my
morals and values about married men went right
out the window just as I was coming out of all of
my clothes. We made love. He was gentle and
took his time. He was also well endowed. What
we shared was beautiful.

The next morning wasn't so beautiful. The
embarrassment and disappointment in both of
us was written all over my face. As I was trying
to ease from under his arm he took my arm and
turned me toward him. I had tears rolling down
my face. He looked at me with a puzzled look,
grabbed me and held me real tight. I cried like a
baby.

After I stopped crying he put his hand under my chin and raised my face to his. He looked in my eyes and said, "I love you and would never want to hurt you. I'm so very sorry. I don't want you to be sad. If this is all about me being married, that's just about all over and done. I want it to be you and me. That's why I was upset when you were telling me about the guy you just met. I don't want you to be with anybody else but me. I finally found you. You are my soul mate. The one I'm destined to be with. Please, just give us a chance." I believed him.

Over the next year William would visit two to three times a week. He told me he had already started making plans to relocate. His wife was back and forth in the house. He assured me they were over and he had filed divorce papers. He even had his attorney call and fax the papers to me to prove he was telling the truth. When he visited we would look at houses and make plans to be married.

I hadn't talked to Sheri or Steve about our plans. They were very religious and I really didn't want to hear a sermon. Sheri called and asked if I wanted to go to Destin, Florida for a girls pamper me weekend. William wouldn't be back until Tuesday and my kids were with their grandparents for the summer so I told her it sounded like a great idea and I would leave heading her way in about an hour. I tried to reach William but couldn't. When Sheri and I went to the spa we never took our cell phones. If there was an emergency Steve could always call the hotel room but he usually never disturbed us for anything.

We arrived at our suite just in time to make it to our massage appointment. As we were getting our massage Sheri said, "Did you hear about William?" I raised my head and said, "What? I just saw I mean spoke to him yesterday." She said, "His wife served him with divorce papers today. As it turns out the gay man wasn't gay. He's her man and they've been seeing each other right under William's nose all this time. He's even been to their house for barbeques and other family functions. I think it serves him right though. He has had so many women on his wife until it ain't even funny. What goes around comes around my momma always said."

I started feeling really sick in my stomach. All I could think was that lying fuck. Sheri kept talking, "She's not going to get anything from him though. The house is in her name and was given to her by her father. William lost his job a couple of months ago. He got caught in a hotel room with one of the firm's clients smoking marijuana. You know he was doing her too." I couldn't take anymore. I told Sheri I was going to the room because my stomach was queasy from the lunch I had on the road.

I couldn't get to the room fast enough. I ran to the bathroom and kept throwing up for what seemed like forever. When Sheri came back to the room I was laying on the bed with a cold towel over my face. She took one look at me and said, "You don't look so good." I said, "I feel horrible. I think I've got food poisoning. I think I better go home." That wasn't it but I had to tell her something.

I went down to the front desk to pay my portion of the bill. I had to go back to the room to get my things. As I was approaching the door of the hotel room, I heard Sheri on the phone. She was talking to Steve. She said, "Yeah, I got to give it to her. She played it off like a pro. Yeah, I told her everything, poor baby. Yeah. I think she'll be okay. I hate to be William right now. He's catching it from every which way." I made a noise at the door and Sheri hung up the phone. I said, "I thought I heard you on the phone." Sheri replied, "Yeah. That was Steve. He said William was looking for you and wanted to know if he should give him the number here. I told him he better not. You don't want to hear all that crying. You don't feel good." I just said, "Thanks. I'll talk to you when you get home." Sheri and I said goodbye and I was on my way back home.

When I turned onto my street I could see William's car parked in front of my house. He had a small U-Haul trailer attached. I stopped the car and called the police. The police came to make him leave the area. He was outside his car screaming, "Just give me a chance to explain." I ignored him as I walked toward the house. As I was opening the door I heard William say, "Fuck you then, you lame ass bitch." I got a restraining order. I later found out the attorney that called me was a friend of William and the divorce papers he had shown me were fake.

I heard from William eighteen months after the day the police forced him to leave from in front of my house. I was at work. The department secretary came to my door and said there was an important call from a hospital holding for me. I panicked; my children, my parents. I picked up the phone and said, "Hello." Tears were already forming in the wells of my eyes. The person on the other end said, "Please don't hang up. It's William." He was calling from a drug rehabilitation hospital. I looked at the phone in amazement. I didn't hang up. I didn't say anything. He said, "Hello, are you there?" I cleared my throat and said, "Yes." He said, "I just wanted to call you to tell you how sorry I am for the way I treated you. I'm in therapy now. I had a lot of issues to deal with. You broke my heart and I started using drugs." I hung up the phone and have never heard from him again.

Insight

I thought I was on the right path. After my divorce I chose to be celibate, to love me. I wanted to take time to evaluate me and understand what I wanted in a man. When I met William I was happy and content. I had beautiful children who were doing well in school and other aspects of their lives, loving and supportive parents, and a fulfilling career. In the beginning William was a great friend. He became someone I could confide in. He was a welcomed addition to my life. We laughed, had wonderful conversations and great fun together.

Sheri and Steve tried to warn me but I didn't want to see or hear what they were saying. I closed my eyes and allowed this man to turn my world upside down. He was married and I chose to ignore the fact he was someone else's. If I had not been there, listening to William's complaints about his marriage, maybe his wife could have been there. Whether I want to admit it or not I inserted myself into their marriage. I was the third party in the marriage, the temptation that allowed William to justify his infidelities. No, I did not push him into committing adultery but whenever he and his wife had a problem he knew he could call me. I was his "friend". I was having a relationship with William without having a relationship. I believe it just made it easier for him not to deal with whatever problems he was facing in his marriage.

By the time William and I became involved in a sexual relationship I thought no more about his marriage. I wanted him for myself. I wanted us. I allowed myself to be fooled into thinking what I was doing was okay. William hurt me in the worst way. After William, it felt like my heart had been ground in a meat grinder three times over.   Whenever I think about William, I remember what Sheri said at the spa that day. What goes around comes around. I don't think I deserved what William did to me but I can't ignore my foolishness in the whole ordeal either. I went from being supportive of William to being selfish and wanting William for myself. I wanted someone else's man, someone else's husband. I cried a long time after my affair with William and that's just what it was an affair, a sexual relationship between two people not married to each other, nothing withstanding. It could have never been anything more.

Keith - The Empathy Man

Keith was a dreamer and could get anyone charged on an idea. What was amazing was his intoxicating presentation of an idea. I am sure you've known people who can sell a nun a getaway package to a nude beach without blinking an eye. That was Keith. Keith is an average looking guy, almost six feet tall, and a muscular build. His personality makes him cuter than he really is. When he finished high school he went into the army. After completing four years, he was honorably discharged and took up hustling for a living. He sold CD's, DVD's, competed in Karaoke competitions, and was the deejay at a small neighborhood club every Thursday, Friday and Saturday. When he was in a crowd he commanded all attention and kept everyone laughing.

Keith's father died before he was born. His mother died shortly after the birth of his brother. He and his brother, Casey, grew up in the foster care system. Keith had lived in seven foster homes until he was seventeen. Between him and his brother they lived in a total of sixteen different homes. They lost touch during their teen years but reconnected when Keith was twenty-three. After Keith aged out of the foster care system he searched for his brother for over a year before he found him. They had been very close ever since they reunited. Keith is the oldest so he was always looking out for his younger brother. You wouldn't have guessed Keith had gone through such traumatic experiences by talking to him. You hardly ever saw him in a bad mood or mad about anything. He never felt sorry for himself and should have coined the phrase "when the going gets tough, the tough get going". He practically used it on a daily basis. Simply put, his middle name should have been Mr. Resilient.

I met Keith on a Thursday night. Some of the women at work decided to stop at the neighborhood bar and asked if I wanted to come along. I had never gone out with them but decided I would go. I didn't have anything planned. I was new at work. What could it hurt? Maybe I would make new friends. All of my closest girlfriends were married with children and lived far away. Most nights I would just sit at home by myself, doing nothing.

The club was small but very cute. Each table had a red phone on it. If someone wanted to speak to you from another table he/she could call your phone by dialing the number of your table and ask if you wanted to dance, a drink, or if they could come over to talk to you. When you picked up the phone it displayed where the call was coming from but you still had to locate which table corresponded to the number appearing on the phone. I thought different but cute. There was hardly anyone in the club when we got there but as the night went on it was jam packed with people. Keith came in around 7:00 p.m. It was if the Pope himself walked in. Men and women were clamoring all over him. All I could think was who is he? And what makes him so special?

When he hit the DJ booth the party started. Excitement was in the air. Everyone was having a great time. Just as I was finishing my second gin and tonic, the little red phone rang. By this time the girls and I were extremely giddy. We looked at the phone and around the room trying to figure out who was calling. We laughed hysterically about who was going to answer it. Maybe it was the man with the womanish hips, or the guy still wearing a Gheri curl, or the old guy with the tight polyester pants. We couldn't stop laughing. The rings stopped and started again. I finally picked it up. It was Keith. No wonder we couldn't see who was calling. The call was coming from the DJ booth. Just as I picked up the phone Keith said, "Hey you sexy motherfucker", just as he was putting on Prince. I slammed the phone down. That was some ignorant shit. I stayed a few more minutes, got my coat and headed for the door. Just as I was approaching my car I heard "Hey! Hey! Excuse me pretty lady. Please let me apologize for my rudeness." I turned around and it was Keith. I said, "It's okay" and unlocked my car door. As I was closing the door Keith was still talking. I drove off. Let his ignorant ass talk to the wind.

When I returned to work the next day, each of my new found friends had a Keith story. Oh he is so funny. He kept asking about you all night. He even bribed them by buying two more rounds of drinks if they would promise to bring me back to the club. This went on for the rest of the day. It was Keith this and Keith that.

All except for the ignorant phone call, I had a good time and had already planned to go back to the club. My co-workers and I met there every Thursday after work. Over the next five months, Keith tried everything from telling jokes to giving me free CD's and DVD's to dedicating songs to me. He would say "and this is for the mean one" and point at me. I had to give it to him he was persistent.

Now this attention, however unwanted in the beginning, made me feel desired. But, as time went on, it was doing nothing for that feeling that pushes you into doing something you probably know you shouldn't but can't help doing. Yes, I was horny as hell and had an urge that could no longer be satisfied by me. You know what I mean.

Although I usually only have two drinks, this particular night I was on my fourth. We didn't have to work the next day because it was

Christmas Eve. My family was getting together on Saturday, Christmas Day, so I would have all day Friday to recuperate if needed. I was dancing and having a great time. When I returned to the table, I asked my girlfriends to watch my purse until I went to the restroom. When I opened the door of the restroom to go back to my table, Keith was standing there with a present. He grabbed my hand and pulled me down into a dark corner. He said, "This is for you. I hope you like it." I said, "No, Keith I can't accept it. I didn't..." I couldn't get the rest of what I was trying to say to him out because he pulled me close and kissed me. And I kissed him back. At the end of the kiss he said, "Just take it and stop being so mean." I said, "O.K." I sat in my seat the rest of the night thinking about that kiss.

I had just left a really bad relationship, the kind that ties your stomach up in knots whenever you think about it. I had been pushed, shoved, hit, and made to feel worthless. It was a relationship I thought I would never be in. My ex and I were together for three years. He was a successful businessman. Truthfully, the emotional abuse was there from the beginning. I may not have recognized it right off but it was apparent after a while. The physical abuse started during the last year of our relationship. I stayed because I loved him and wanted to fix him, me, and us. I stayed because I was weak for a man who couldn't love me back.

After that, I honestly wasn't looking for a serious relationship and I was never one to sleep around. As a matter of fact, I had never slept with anyone who I wasn't in a relationship with. I was very serious about this to the point that I never slept with anyone until after six months of dating.

Keith was definitely not my type. He had shown how ignorant he could be. My heart had been broken and I was being very careful I didn't enter into a relationship that would end up like the last one. I didn't think my heart could stand it. I even moved to another state to start all over. You see, when I loved I loved hard. I was all in. And when I fell, the crash and shattering of my heart could be heard from miles around. I made up in my mind the next relationship I chose to enter into had to be with someone who believed in protecting and cherishing my love as much as I did his.

Anyway, I went home and decided to open the gift. Inside the box was a pretty buttery yellow cashmere sweater. It was beautiful, not my size, but beautiful all the same. I guess since it was a sweater I could wear it a little bigger. I couldn't understand why he thought he could shop at Avenue for me. I was a size 12 not 18. The sweater was so pretty. I didn't want to give it back. If it didn't work out re-gifting was always an option. Inside the box was a card. On the card Keith had written all of his phone numbers and a message asking me to call him sometime. The horny monster inside of me was saying - Call him! Call him now! My mind said - Stop it and go to sleep.

The next day I just sat around, wrapped gifts for my family, and watched my favorite Christmas movie, 'It's a Wonderful Life'. The house phone rang. It was one of the girls from work. She told me she gave my cell phone number to Keith since it was the giving season and she didn't think I would mind. I was furious. I got off the phone and checked my cell phone. Six missed calls, all from Keith. Just as I was laying the phone on the table it vibrated, Keith again. I answered. It was apparent the calls were not going to stop. To be perfectly honest I was glad he was calling and I wanted to talk to him.

I felt like a psycho. One minute I was pissed he had my phone number and the next I was dying to answer his call. I said, "Hello." Keith responded, "Happy almost Christmas. How are you today?" I replied, "Fine." Keith said, "Oh I know that." All I could think was please not that tired old line. There was dead air. Keith said, "What you doing?" I told him. He asked if I had opened the gift. I told him I had and the sweater was beautiful. We made small talk for a while and then Keith asked if he could come by for a few minutes. He wanted to show me something and ask my opinion about it. I wasn't doing much so I said, "O.K." I gave him my address, started straitening up, took a shower and had a long conversation with my conscience. I had beaten the urge the night before and was rather proud of myself. I kept talking to myself. Just because he was coming over did not mean anything physical had to happen. What we shared was just a kiss. Besides I didn't even like Keith like that.

When he arrived, he looked kind of upset. I had never seen him like this before. He did have a serious side. He came in and told me his birth mother had contacted him. I was confused. I distinctly remember Keith telling a group of people both his parents were deceased in between him telling jokes about incidents that happened to him in different foster homes. Well it seems his mother was alive and well and living in Virginia with her husband and three children. I was out done. How could this be true? I read the letter she sent him.

Apparently, she paid a woman for the use of her medical card and identification. The woman listed on Keith and his brother's birth certificates was a drug addict and not their biological mother. She said she tried very hard to keep things together after Keith's father died. After she found out she was pregnant with Keith's brother things got worst. She was twenty-two years old with two small children, no job and no one to turn to. She didn't have a permanent address so it was difficult to get public assistance. She thought giving Keith and Casey to the state was the best thing she could do for them at the time. She planned to get herself together and go back to get her children. About a month after she left them at the police station, she walked into the child welfare office and asked what she needed to do to get her children back. They had no record of her. She was not on the birth certificates. The caseworker notes stated an unknown woman brought two young boys to the police station at 3:00 a.m. and refused to give her name. Keith and his brother were asleep and never woke up. She had given them cough syrup to make sure they stayed asleep. She tried to explain the situation but the caseworker was very mean to her and threatened to charge her with fraud. She was young and scared and didn't realize she had alternatives available to her. She believed it was too late. She and her best friend decided to leave the state and start new lives. Keith's mother now had Leukemia and wanted to right all the wrongs in her life before she died.

After I read the letter, I was just sitting there looking as dumb founded as Keith. This was way too heavy. I went to the kitchen and made two very stiff drinks. We drank them and agreed he needed to talk to his brother. He needed to give himself time to think about what she was asking and how he truly felt. Keith noticed the paused movie I was watching. We decided to have another drink, pop popcorn, and finish looking the movie.

Just as the movie was ending Keith leaned over and kissed me. Danger! Danger! Conscience where are you? The kiss was long and good. He started caressing my body and I returned the favor. Against my very strict rule of waiting to having sexual intercourse with a man until you've dated at least six months, I willingly followed as Keith led me to my bedroom. There was a mixture of my pain, his hurt, his hurt, my pain, the horny monster, and a man's six-month lust. We did not emerge until the next day at three o'clock. Just enough time for me to shower, gather my gifts and head to my family's house.

My parents had flown in late the night before. It was going to be great to see my mom and dad. I thought about Keith. He was just sitting on the couch watching me prepare. I asked, "What do you have planned today?" He replied, "Nothing. My brother went to Vegas with some of his buddies." I knew I shouldn't have but it was Christmas. I asked Keith if he wanted to spend the holiday with my family. He was ecstatic. I gave him the address. I told him he would have to go home and change into a shirt and tie. He arrived right before dinner was served so no one was able to give him the third degree before dinner. However, during dinner was another story. The charismatic guy, you know the one who has women and men falling all over themselves to be in his presence, showed up. He kept everyone entertained. I barely got to talk to him. My mother and aunt were already discussing how our children might look.

We started dating after that. My mother and aunt checked in weekly on our status. They were so looking forward to planning a wedding. We were nowhere near that point, which I told them every week, but they insisted they would continue to monitor our progress. I dared not tell them neither of us was thinking about marriage or that we were just kind of doing something with no real definition of what it was.

About four months later, I went with Keith and his brother to meet their mother. Keith looked so much like her. She had to be telling the truth. It was a very strained visit. His mother had not told her husband about Keith and his brother until well after she had been diagnosed with Leukemia. Her husband was very cold and standoffish. Their brother and two sisters knew what was going on and were nice but still skeptical. I don't think they knew how to respond to the situation. They were only thirteen and fifteen. Keith seemed to accept what his mother said and remained in touch with her until she passed. His younger brother, Casey, wanted nothing to do with her and was very angry. He wouldn't comment on any conversation surrounding her or their past lives in foster care. He did, however, accept half of the $20,000 she willed to them.

Keith had so many plans, ideas, and dreams. He wasn't exactly sure what he wanted to do with the money so he put his half in the bank and did not touch it. Casey, on the other hand, seemed to blow his inheritance in a matter of weeks. Time went on and Keith and I were okay. We never argued, we had fun together, and the sex was phenomenal. All that hurt and pain tangled up in a big ball of sweaty lust was always extraordinary. We had what one might call a pleasant pleasure seeking relationship. We seemed to be in a state of constant progression and healing. We talked about our feelings, past hurt, pain and heartache. Mine mostly centered around my last relationship while his focused on his childhood. Although he joked about it in public his experiences in foster care were definitely not a joking matter. I felt for him. I admired his fight to survive. I adored his sincerity and concern for how and what I was feeling. We were good.

As time went on there were fewer conversations about our pasts. We began to talk about the present and future. We had helped each other to evolve. We were happy and moving on. I got a promotion to a very high administrative position at work. Keith used the money his mother left him and his savings to invest in a dollar store franchise. We became real friends. We had changed. We were very busy with our new responsibilities so we were seeing less and less of each other. Most of our contact was via phone or email.

Even when we were together we were so tired. Our time spent together began to consist of having a drink, watching a movie, and falling asleep on the couch. It wasn't until we both realized we had not had sex in over a month and neither of us was even thinking about it that we began to reevaluate our relationship. We had never even discussed us forever. It had never been in the equation for us. We decided we would always remain friends but it was best we both move on. We were each stronger now and could do that. We still talked every day. We talked about everything even dates we had been on. Those were some of the funniest stories we shared.

One day I was in my office and my administrative assistant came in to let me know Keith was in the waiting room and wanted to see me. I told him to show him in. When he came in I could tell there was something wrong. He told me he had just gotten a call from the hospital. Casey was in a car accident and he needed to go the hospital right away. He wanted me to go with him. We got to the hospital just as they were taking Casey into surgery. Apparently, a car full of teenager's ditched school, got high, and hit Casey head on.

While we were in the waiting room my cousin Charlotte ran in crying hysterically. I grabbed her in my arms to console her. She blurted out "Is Casey going to be okay? I'm pregnant and we're supposed to get married."

What? When did all this happen? I had never
known Charlotte to date anyone. There were
family rumors she might be a lesbian. I couldn't
talk. Keith told Charlotte everything we knew.
Charlotte just cried and cried. The doctor came
in a long while later and told us Casey was going
to be fine. He had a couple of broken ribs, a
broken arm and leg, and a lot of bruising. We
were all so happy. Keith just fell to his knees
and began to sob. I felt his pain and then I
started. Charlotte became the pillar of strength
and took care of both of us. By the time we went
to see Casey we had gotten ourselves together.

I knew Casey had been through a
traumatic experience but I couldn't help myself.
I had to know. Apparently, Charlotte and Casey
were secretly dating for over a year. They met at
a friend's wedding. Charlotte knew how the
family pressured us to marry. We had one
cousin on her fourth marriage trying to please
the family. Charlotte didn't want anyone
interfering in her relationship. Surprisingly,
Charlotte had many relationships none of us
knew about. Casey stayed in the hospital for
two weeks. Ten months later, Casey and
Charlotte married.

Keith started dating Brandy, a woman he
met on one of his business trips. I was dating
Carl, an Executive at my company's main office.
We were all at the wedding. It was as always.
My family loved Keith. Carl and Brandy seemed
a bit out of place. Carl took it much better than

Brandy. Keith had to do a lot of convincing to
see her again. Carl and I continued to date. As
time went on, Carl and I became closer. After
some serious pleading and begging on Keith's
part, so did Keith and Brandy.

Keith called one day to ask me to meet
him for drinks at the club where we first met. I
declined. I did not want to feed the rumor mill
at work and put Carl or myself in that position.
We met at my apartment. Keith was looking
very serious. I asked what was wrong. He told
me he loved Brandy and had asked her to marry
him. I thought that was great news but why was
he looking so down. He told me she said no
because she believed he was in love with me. I
couldn't help it. I laughed and laughed and
laughed some more. I told him Carl had a hard
time with our relationship at first but now he is
totally cool with it. He said, "It's not funny and
I'm serious. I'm going to have to make a
decision. I love you as a friend but I love her as
a woman and I don't want to lose her."

Are you kidding me? After all we've been
through. I was pissed. I told him, "Well it looks
like you've made your decision. Now get your
punk ass out of my house." Carl came by that
night. He was in the bathroom looking in the
mirror. I was standing outside of the door. I
could see his reflection. I told him what Keith
said and how upset and pissed I was. I told him
I put Keith out of the apartment. I could not
believe my eyes. He was clinching his fist and

silently saying, "Yes! Yes!" I slung the door open. The door hit him in the head. I said, "I saw you." At first he laughed but soon became very serious. He began to talk. He explained how difficult a thing it was to know your woman had a serious relationship with their now so-called friend. He said, "No man wants to be best friends with his woman's ex man, a man who has been everywhere he's been." He also expressed how hard it was to comply with what Keith and I were asking of him and Brandy. He said he was glad what was between Keith and I was over and maybe now he and I could move forward in our relationship. I never knew Carl felt this way. Whenever he was around Keith they seemed to be having a great time. All I knew was Keith was my friend and I never thought it would be any other way. Carl asked how I would deal with it if I were on the other side. I thought about that statement. It really made me see how selfish I was. I understood.

I called Keith the next day and apologized. Keith and Brandy got married the next year. Carl and I married two years later. I never contact Keith. Every now and then I'll get a call from Keith asking how everything is going or I'll see him at a family function since his brother is married to my cousin. Brandy is always very nice and cordial but something deep inside of me hates her guts. So I'm phony with her to keep the peace.

Although sometimes I miss Keith very much I respect his wishes. I think I will always love Keith. He was the conduit to my survival and to the person I am today. Carl and I have three children and a wonderful life. I wouldn't change a thing. Keith seems very happy and has two little boys named Keith, Jr. and Brandon. I know things worked out for the best but I still miss my friend sometimes.

Insight

Sometimes life kicks us so hard we wonder how we will ever get up. When Keith and I met we were both broken and filled with a lot of pain. We found each other. We were empathetic towards each other. We understood each other because we both had experiences that caused us a lot of hurt and grief. I once asked Keith why he pursued me the way he did in the beginning. He answered, "There was something about you that wouldn't let me rest until I knew you."

I often think about the old adage that says something about people coming into your life for a reason, a season or a lifetime. Somewhere deep down I always knew there was a reason for Keith but in the end I wanted it to be for a lifetime. I wanted his presence in my life to be the way I defined it without any consideration of how our relationship affected others in our lives. I wanted it to be the way I wanted it to be. He became my security blanket. Things didn't work out the way I had envisioned but it is definitely better to have known Keith than to not have known him at all.

I will have to be satisfied with the way things are. And I am. We made it through. We're at the place many struggle to get to. We set our sights on finding loving relationships, having wonderful children, successful careers and creating and extending supportive families. We have achieved those things.

In life you take the good with the bad. You make the difficult decisions. You hurt, you cry, you laugh, you're up and you're down. In the end, you cherish each of those experiences and pray when it's all said and done you've done your best.

Sometimes we have Keith's in our lives and we try to hold on to them. We try to change the ending even when we know the beginning. Instead of accepting our experiences for what they are we want and try to change the experience or even the outcome of those experiences. In doing so we put roadblocks up that inhibit us from moving forward and being in a position to receive the good life has in store for us. It is so very difficult to identify those learning/teaching experiences that happen only to make us stronger in order that we might be prepared for the next thing in our life. Keith and I always knew forever never included us together. Facing it, no matter how difficult, was the best thing we could have done for each other. I am so proud of us.

KENDRA

Brian - The Uh Huh Now Back to Me Man

Brian is an educated man with four degrees and has an argument for every subject matter in the world. He is very handsome in a scholarly kind of way. He is 6'3, has a deep heavy voice, and a very broad and distinctive chin. He is very health conscience and takes excellent care of his body. He's always going to the doctor for one reason or the other. He's the man that will inspire you to make your yearly visits to the doctor, stop eating pork, exercise and consider becoming a vegetarian. As he always said, in that low monotone sexy voice, "Your body is a temple entrusted to you by God, you only have one. What are you going to say on judgment day when God asks did you take care of the temple, the likeness of me?"

I met Brian at a conference on the impact of parental mental illness on children, families and communities. We began talking and hit it off immediately. During the conference, we went to the same conference sessions, ate together and enjoyed much of the nightlife with our colleagues. Instantly, we knew we would be friends for a long time.

We were interested in many of the same things and I must admit it was quite refreshing to talk to a man who could stimulate my mind and talk on a wide range of subject matters. I was always anxious to talk to him. He had so many real life experiences to talk about. Experiences I had not encountered. He was intelligent and interesting. He was an excellent orator and wrote some of the most beautiful poetry. The words that came from his mouth soothed your soul and lulled your mind into a sort of chaotic peace. His thoughts were deep. He made you want to stop and examine each breath you took and the meaning of it.

We talked every day, sometimes two to three times a day. I was always excited to hear about his day. There was always some fantastic story he could share. He would also tell me about his personal life. He had never been married but had a live-in girlfriend of eight years and a two-year-old son. His girlfriend had recently left him, taken their son with her, and moved fifteen hundred miles away. When I asked why she left, he would only say she complained there was no room for her and the baby in his life. I really couldn't get a fix on what that statement meant but unfortunately would find out.

It seemed as though he didn't mind the breakup of the relationship but was furious his ex would move so far away, making it difficult for him to see his son on a regular basis. He went to see several attorneys. He wasn't willing to take sole custody of his son but wanted the court to make his ex move in closer proximity of him so he and his son could maintain regular contact. I didn't think he had a leg to stand on. His ex had told him about her impending move over a year ago. Her company was relocating. He admitted his ex was a good mother. Basically, each of the attorney's he spoke to told him the same thing I told him. He didn't have a leg to stand on.

I told Brian during several conversations to try to be accepting of the situation and supportive of his ex. I was sure moving to a new state, with a young child and no family support was difficult for her. I thought they could work things out in a way that would best benefit their son and satisfy each of their needs. It was if he hadn't heard a word I said. I chalked it up to him not coming to terms with the breakup and really missing his son and whether he wanted to admit it or not his ex.

As time went, on we continued our talks and meetings at different conferences. Both of our careers were taking off. I had received two promotions in two years. He had left his job to start his own business. He became a motivational speaker. He had bookings all over the country and had made two television appearances on two different talk shows. Of course, as success came closer in reach for both of us, office politics and other roadblocks reared their ugly heads. The backstabbers and haters seemed to come out of nowhere.

Mostly, I talked with my best friend at work about the goings on at work and Brian talked to me. I needed a break. I planned to take a week off of work to clear my mind so I could return to work refreshed and ready to deal with the crap going on at my job. I told Brian about my plans and he invited me to meet him at a conference happening in a small city about an hour away from where I lived. I thought this would be great. I would finally get a chance to see him at work.

I was sitting in the audience waiting for him to make his appearance. For some strange reason I was anxious and nervous. Not for myself but for him. I hoped he would do well. When he began to speak all of the nervous energy I was trying so hard to contain melted away. The words came from his mouth like they were meant for only him to speak.

No matter who you were before you walked into that room you were elevated to a place of serenity and peace, a place of joy, a place of self-examination. The atmosphere allowed you to be okay with who you were. Suddenly you had the ability to hone in on your purpose and the need of the universe for you to fulfill that purpose. It was if you had been elevated in status by God himself and now you knew your responsibility of maintaining order and goodness. It was if you were suddenly aware of your responsibility to future generations. Not in the broad sense or the disconnected use of the words "future generations" but in a way that allowed you to really tap into your sense of responsibility to your descendants while also allowing you to visit and appreciate the gifts received by you from your ancestors.

He was truly gifted. In our isolated conversations I only experienced a very minute glimpse into this man. Sitting there and listening to what he was saying and seeing who he was gave me a whole new perspective. I felt privileged to even know him. After his presentation, he stopped to talk to anyone who struck up a conversation with him. It was almost two hours after his presentation before we were able to leave the venue.

We decided to go to the hotel and check in. When we arrived there was only one room reserved in his name. He was angry at the conference organizers for not having reserved two rooms for him. He called the contact person to ask if there were any two rooms available at another hotel. It was a small town and had only three hotels. Each of the hotels was booked because of the conference. I told him I would drive back home after we ate dinner. I was starving. He seemed really disappointed.

He checked in and we went to his room. I watched television while he showered and changed clothes in the bathroom. By the time we left, many of the restaurants were closed. We ended up at a small bar and grill. The food was really good. I had a couple of glasses of wine and he had flavored seltzer water. We talked until the place closed. Before we left Brian asked the bartender where we could buy some of the wine I was drinking. He told him the liquor stores were closed but he could sell him a bottle. Brian brought a bottle and we left.

During our conversation at the bar we agreed I would stay in Brian's room for the night. It was late and he wanted to talk more. I didn't think anything of it. We made it back to his room, opened the bottle of wine and talked a little more. I was getting really tired. I told Brian I was going to take a shower and put on my pajamas. When I came out of the bathroom Brian looked at me and burst into laughter. "What do you have on? What are all those little bears and honey jars about?" Brian said. I replied, "Don't talk about my flannels. I love these. They are my favorite. What's so funny about them?" He just shook his head and said, "My, my, my."

While I was showering, Brian had called the front desk and requested a cot. He was lying on the cot and had turned back the covers on the bed. I climbed into the bed. We talked until we both fell asleep. When I woke up in the middle of the night to go to the toilet Brian was on top of the covers next to me in the bed. I was sleepy. I didn't care where he was at that moment. I went to the bathroom, came back, and climbed into bed. Just as I was getting settled into my sleeping position Brian said, "Hey, you." I said, "Hi and closed my eyes." Brian threw his arm over me and pulled me close to him. My back was to him. He held me tight. I just lay there. I was all talked out and couldn't say anything and didn't want to get him started. He lived to talk.

I fell asleep. I was awakened by the heat of Brian's lips kissing my neck and a slow delicate tug on my earlobes with his teeth. I didn't move. Next I felt his strong hand rubbing gently back and forth over my hip. He moved his hand around the front of my body and turned me towards him and passionately kissed me. We made love. Neither of us said a word. We were touching each other in a way that needed no words. There was complete silence except for the heated panting and the sound of kisses we exchanged. It was wonderful. It was erotic. It was innocent. It was pure ecstasy. It was if I instantly fell in love with Brian. It wasn't just the sex. It was more. It was the whole package. Brian showered and dressed while I lay asleep. When I awoke I found a note that said: Sleeping beauty meet me at the conference luncheon at 1:00 p.m.

As I was getting dressed my cell phone rang. It was my best friend from work. She told me I should get back to work because there were some underhanded things going on that could hurt my program. I thanked her, went to the conference luncheon and told Brian I would have to leave after the luncheon. He asked me to call to let him know I arrived safely. I thought about Brian and I all the way home. I called my best girlfriend. We had been friends since high school. I told her all about it, every detail. I was so excited and couldn't wait to see Brian again.

I didn't speak to Brian until three days after I left the conference. I thought about why but couldn't really focus on it with dealing with the mess at work. I knew he had to travel to three different states over the next two days but he had always made time before at the airport, checking into a hotel, during a break at a conference where he was speaking, etc. I tried to chalk it up to him being really busy. I think him not calling and it being in the back of my mind helped me save my program. I was like a bitch on wheels. Nothing was getting past me. I was ferocious. My friend at work said she had never seen me act the way I was before and wondered what was up. I told her about the night I spent with Brian and that I had not heard from him.

Just as I was sharing the details of Brian and my escapade, my cell phone rang. It was Brian. This was strange. The thought of why he was calling now ran across my mind. It was at a time I'm usually not available. I said, "Hello." Brian's response was as if he was surprised to hear my voice. Was he going to leave a message? He said, "Hi. I need to have a serious conversation with you. Do you have time now?" I said, "Of course. I'm on my way to my car. I'll call you right back when I get there."

I called Brian. He began by very briefly expressing how much he cared about me then he went on to talk about what was going on in his life. It took me thirty minutes to get to my house. During those thirty minutes we talked about Brian, his feelings, his work, and his son. As I was walking up the stairs to the entrance of my house, I asked Brain to hold on while I opened the front door. He seemed perturbed because he was in the middle of telling me what happened to him at the last conference where he presented. As soon as I put the phone back to my ear Brian picked up precisely at the point he had left off.

An hour later I was still listening to Brian. I couldn't believe this was what was so important. What about the night we spent together? Didn't he want to talk about that? That's what seemed important to me. I still didn't say anything. When he took a breath, I started telling him what had gone on at work. I could hear pots clanging in the background. I stopped and said, "What are you doing?" He said, "Oh, I'm getting ready to stir fry veggies." I continued with my story. Brian seemed distant, like he wasn't really listening.

After I finished telling him all of the sordid details of the incident at work he said, "Uh-huh." He then proceeded to talk about how he makes his veggie stir-fry, the ingredients, how long he stir fries it, what kind of oil he uses and on and on and on. He had no interest in what I was saying. I was baffled. I told him someone was at the door and I would talk to him later.

After I had composed myself, I called Brian back. I asked him flat out why he didn't even mention the night we spent together. I told him I was not a one-night stand kind of girl and I take my virtue seriously. I also told him I don't have sex with just any ole body. I wanted to know what he was thinking. I wanted to know why he felt only he and what was happening to him was important. I wanted to know why, while he was an excellent speaker, he was a horrible listener.

Brian had the nerve, the audacity to be insulted. He said, "Look, I need someone to support me. I'm trying to do something with my life. God has given me a gift and I want to share it with the world. The little things you go through at work are minuscule in comparison to what I have to deal with on a daily basis. I needed someone at the hotel that night and I'm so glad you were there. I'm not looking to get married. I have a path that has been laid for me and I have to follow it. You have helped me so much. Whenever I need to talk to someone I know I can call on you. You have great insight and I need that. I need someone outside of the field to keep me grounded. If I've hurt you or caused you any pain I'm sorry but I need someone to listen to me."

I almost fell out of my seat. Clarity is a mu'tha. At least he was honest. In a very calm and polite voice I said, "Brian, I never said anything about marriage. In a relationship, friends or otherwise, you have to be able to give as well as get. Now I can clearly see what you want and need. I also see there is a conflict. In the beginning, I only wanted to be your friend. You took it to the next level the night in the hotel room. I don't want to be your fuck buddy and I didn't sign on to be your Muse. To alleviate us parting on bad terms, I think it best we not talk anymore. I wish you well and hope you get everything you want and are destined to have."

Afterwards, I thought I would be upset and cry. I went to the refrigerator and got a bottle of white wine. I put on a CD of love music and sat on the sofa. As I was drinking my wine and listening to the music I began to reflect on Brian and what had transpired. I wanted to be sad about everything. While I was sitting there trying to be sad, I realized I was squinting my eyes trying to make tears come. I burst into laughter and realized how silly the whole thing was. I wasn't upset. I had just moved on.

I have not spoken to Brian since. He tried to call for a short period of time after I told him we should no longer talk. He left several apologetic messages. I wouldn't answer his calls. I figured he'd find someone else to act as his personal savant. One day, after about eighteen months, I received a surprising e-mail from Brian. I was surprised because I changed jobs and had changed my e-mail. I guess you can find just about anyone using the Internet. In the email Brian said he was working hard, his business was doing great and his son had moved closer making visitation much easier. He also said he was still single. All I could think was I wonder why. I never responded.

Insight

There really wasn't room in Brian's life for anyone else but Brian. I was so taken by him. He was smart, driven, handsome, tall, and strong. Yeah, all surface qualities but a ten in every area. However, except for self-confidence, he had not yet mastered the inner qualities, like caring, empathy, sympathy, understanding, compassion, etc. He believed God had set him on a path that required him to use his gift of speech to help people. This may undoubtedly be true but his double mindedness seemed a bit ungodly to me.

I don't hold the night at the hotel against Brian. I could have stopped it at anytime. What I do fault Brian for is his self-righteous attitude that allows him to stand before crowds of people, motivating them to assess themselves, to better themselves while at the same time privately misusing those around him for his own gain. I. I. I. It was all about Brian all the time. He even went so far as to have sex with me to fulfill his immediate needs without any consideration of my feelings and would have continued to do so if I had not stepped away from the situation. Looking back I don't think Brian has the capacity to really care about others feelings. He's like a sociopath, someone whose behaviors are a danger to others. Although he's not a murderer his actions might be considered criminal when it comes to matters of the heart. Brian was probably the greatest masquerader of them all, a wolf in sheep's clothing.

DANA

Walter The Faux Relationship Man

Walter is approximately 5'6, very muscular, has beautiful eyes, and is always very neat and well put together. He has a steady job, which he has worked since he graduated from high school. He's the middle child of five siblings and grew up in a family headed by his mother. When he and his sisters and brothers where very young his father left his mother. He barely remembers him but the lasting effects of abandonment are apparent in Walter. He's nice, always reliable, and the guy everyone likes, men and women alike. When I say everyone, I mean everyone, your mother, father, sister, brother, friends, just everybody.

I met Walter when I was 11 years old. We were at the skating rink. I was in the kiddy skating area. To this day roller-skating has been the one thing I could not master even after trying and trying and falling and trying again. I would usually leave the amateur skating area and watch the experts on the big rink until the dance club opened. This is where I shined. I was watching the skaters jamming on the big rink when I saw this little kid hanging with the best of them. Man he could skate. It made me feel a little incompetent. I wished I could skate half as well as him.

When the dance club opened, I went in and danced until my shirt was soaking wet. I loved it. People would crowd around to see me and an older guy, named Ralph, dance. I loved it. The kid who was on the big rink came up to me while I was taking a break and started talking. He said his name was Walter. I asked him how he got in the dance club. You had to be at least thirteen to get in.

Right the nerve of me. He probably got in the same way I did. Ralph owned the dance floor. I never had a problem getting in after the first day I snuck in and danced with Ralph. Ralph and I were like a main attraction. Like me, maybe Walter knew someone to get him in or maybe he snuck in too. Walter said he was twelve. I couldn't believe it. I thought he was much younger. As we continued to talk, we realized we lived a couple of blocks away from each other. We had never met because I went to private school and the houses we lived in sat on large lots of land so you wouldn't have seen each other in the neighborhood unless you walked the streets everyday.

We talked and laughed the rest of the night in between Ralph and me dancing. I did dance with Walter once though. He said his older brother had taught him how to step and he could show me how. He showed me how and from that night on, all of the steppers songs were reserved for Walter.

We became the best of friends. He was like one of the family and I was like one of his family members. We would go to the park, candy store, bike riding, walking, and talk on the phone for hours. I can't really recount how it occurred but one day we became girlfriend and boyfriend. I was twelve and he was thirteen. This lasted all of two weeks. At that age that's a lifetime. We broke up after he decided he wanted an older girl named Nasty Nita to be his girlfriend. We called her Nasty Nita because she was known to be easy. I really didn't care. I wasn't going to have sex with him so I just said okay. We remained friends and very close. I would tell him about my boyfriends and he would tell me about his girlfriends. This continued throughout high school and college.

We became like real brother and sister. We were at each other's house all the time in high school and school breaks during college. Our mothers would always ask each of us how the other was doing. It always felt like our parents expected us to become a couple and get married. Yeah, we loved each other but it was definitely like brother and sister. This subtle pressure continued well into our thirties. We both married other people in our early twenties. We remained close. His wife didn't appreciate our close relationship at all but my husband didn't mind and Walter was welcome at our house any time.   By age 35 and 36, we were both divorced.

After our divorces, we were looking for that calm, truthful, uncomplicated relationship. We talked for hours about the type of partners we wanted when a big bright light came on.   We realized we were describing each other.   Why not? Maybe we had wasted a lot of time. What we wanted and believed could satisfy our every need could be right in front of our faces.   We decided to take it really slow and not tell anyone until we were sure we would work.   We didn't want the influence of family and friends intruding on our decisions.

We lived in separate states so we planned to visit each other as often as we could. We were only two hours away so this was not a real issue.   At first, the change in our relationship felt really strange.   On one hand, the comfort level at which you converse, divulge intimate secrets and talk about true feelings with your good male friend is definitely compromised when he becomes your love interest.   On the other hand, he knows things about you no one else knows and still loves and accepts you for who you are which could be the missing ingredient that could lead to happiness forever and ever.

Walter and I had been friends for over twenty years.   We liked doing some of the same things.   We enjoyed clubs, restaurants, movies, and shopping.   We always had a great time together. Most of the time, we were like we had

always been.   Although we had committed
ourselves to each other exclusively we chose not
to have sex until we both felt really sure about
what we were doing. We had kissed and it was
nice.   We loved each other.   Of course the
conversation of sexual intercourse had to come
up sooner or later. Each of us had hinted about
it but agreed when the time was right we would
know it.

We decided to take a weekend trip to a
little bed and breakfast in Georgia. The place
was absolutely beautiful. The weather was just
right.   There was a warm gentle breeze with a
hint of gardenia in the air. We checked in, took
our things to our room and decided to do a little
sightseeing. We found a small restaurant not far
from the bed and breakfast and decided to go
back to our room, relax for a while, have some
wine, and return later for dinner.

We had the best time. The restaurant was
cozy, dark and romantic.   The food was
absolutely delicious. And the fragrant wine was
like an aphrodisiac.   The more we drank the
more relaxed we were and the more we talked
about how much we loved each other and how
we didn't want the night to end.

The restaurant was only a few blocks away
from the bed and breakfast. We decided to have
a cup of coffee and walk back to our room. We
hugged and kissed all the way back to the room.
There was no question. The uncertainty of when
and where we would first have sex was put to

rest. It took us about an hour to make it back to the room. We couldn't keep our hands and lips off of each other. We even stopped under a tree, looked at the moon and stars, and kissed for what seemed like forever. It was absolutely beautiful.

We made it to the room. Walter decided to take another shower. I turned on the television and started watching "Love and Basketball" with Sanaa Lathan and Omar Epps. Walter came out of the shower with just his towel on. He still had beads of water rolling down his chest. He walked around the chair I was sitting in and began to kiss me on my neck while at the same time easing the remote from my hand and turning the television off. He took my hand and guided me to stand up. He was now standing behind me, holding me around my waist and whispering in my ear, "Tonight, ok?" I reached back and move his face in front of mine and kissed him. We moved to the bed. Just as he was laying back and pulling me onto him he hit the side of his head on the bedpost. We both ignored it. Then somehow I stubbed my toe on the nightstand. We stopped, looked at each other and burst into laughter. We just lay there, cuddled and fell asleep.

I was fast asleep when a gentle stroke through my hair and very soft and sweet kiss woke me. As dawn began a new day, we started kissing and continued where we left off the previous night. At first, I wondered why he didn't talk much at all until I remembered I always told him how I hated it when guys talked too much in bed. I didn't want to hear what he could do and how he could take me there. I wanted him to be Nike and just do it.

A few minutes later, I started to get a strange and almost creepy feeling as I became more and more naked in front of Walter. As we began to make love I started to feel nauseous. Oh My God, I was freaking out. There was something terribly wrong. I felt like I was in an incestuous relationship. I felt really sick. In my mind, I planned to turn over and pretend to be asleep as soon as he finished. I couldn't even look at him. What was wrong with me? I couldn't hurt Walter. Could he tell I wasn't into it? Did he care? Finally, he was done. I just wanted to lie there in silence.

What? He was ready again. Under any other circumstance this would have been truly a blessing. After the sixth time he was finally through. The last time he climbed on top of me, I was unconsciously making an uncontrollable grunting noise. Walter asked if I was o.k. I realized I was making the awful noise. I could only reply, "Yep". I could not tell him I was totally disgusted, I felt like I had just slept with my brother, we couldn't work, and I loved him and was afraid I would lose his friendship. So I bottled it up and held it in and apparently it came out as a grunting noise.

We left the bed and breakfast later that afternoon. Neither of us did much talking. I think he knew there was something wrong. We dropped the rental car off and went our separate ways at the airport. I cried most of the trip back. Walter didn't call and I didn't call him for about two weeks after our trip. I just couldn't take it anymore. He was my best male friend, like the brother I never had.

I broke down and called him and acted like nothing happened. He did too. To this day we have never talked about the day we had sex or the period of time we were dating. There are no words. We are back to normal. We are like brother and sister. We tell each other everything.

Since then Walter married and divorced two more times. Walter believes if a man impregnates a woman he must marry her. Because his dad left his mother Walter marries. His marriages have left him with two divorces, one annulment, and paying child support. He had two children with his first wife. He later found out the second child wasn't his but continues to pay child support. He caught his second wife in bed with another woman and his third wife claimed to be pregnant when she wasn't. I guess you can say Walter is kind of an easy target for the woman looking for a meal ticket. You see Walter likes a fast woman but he's not quick, swift or slick so he gets taken. Walter married the first and third time because of a pregnancy and his second wife because he was lonely. He married because of pregnancy and not because he loved the women first.

I am dating but I have given up on going after the serious relationship. I date and enjoy life. I'm satisfied with my professional and personal life for the first time in a very long time. Although we never talk about that period in our lives, we sometimes kid about neither of us having anyone when we're old and having to live together for companionship.

Insight

In retrospect we should have never chanced losing or destroying something so very precious to both of us. We were lonely and reckless with our friendship. The consequences of our actions could have turned out so very different. There are stories of best friends riding off into the sunset and living happily ever after but there are also stories of destroyed friendships. We were able to salvage our friendship by pretending nothing ever happened. What we did will leave a stain on our relationship forever. No matter how we pretend. There is no quick fix to finding love or the one you want to spend the rest of your life with.

Walter's the guy everyone loves. He is attentive, caring, respectful, sensitive, and responsible. I know there is someone out there for Walter but that someone isn't me. We're too close. Like brother and sister. That's the way it should stay, like brother and sister.

About the Author

Shonda K. Lawrence, PhD., has enjoyed teaching at several universities and colleges over the past years. She does not consider herself an expert in the area of relationships but wanted to share these short stories about love and relationships. She has two children and lives in Chicopee, Massachusetts.

CPSIA information can be obtained at www.ICGtesting.com
264422BV00004B/12/P